CONTENTS

To the Student

You probably talk at an average rate of about 150 words a minute. If you are a reader of average ability, you read at a rate of about 250 words a minute. So your reading speed is nearly twice as fast as your speaking or listening speed. This example shows that reading is one of the fastest ways to get information.

The purpose of this book is to help you increase your reading rate and understand what you read. The 25 lessons in this book will also give you practice in reading science articles and in preparing for tests in which you must read and understand nonfiction passages within a certain time limit.

Reading Faster and Better

Following are some strategies that you can use to read the articles in each lesson.

Previewing

Previewing before you read is a very important step. This helps you to get an idea of what a selection is about and to recall any previous knowledge you have about the subject. Here are the steps to follow when previewing.

Read the title. Titles are designed not only to announce the subject but also to make the reader think. Ask yourself questions such as What can I learn from the title? What thoughts does it bring to mind? What do I already know about this subject?

Read the first sentence. If they are short, read the first two sentences. The opening sentence is the writer's opportunity to get your attention. Some writers announce what they hope to tell you in the selection. Some writers state their purpose for writing; others just try to get your attention.

Read the last sentence. If it is short, read the final two sentences. The closing sentence is the writer's last chance to get ideas across to you. Some writers repeat the main idea once more. Some writers draw a conclusion—this is what they have been leading up to. Other writers summarize their thoughts; they tie all the facts together.

Skim the entire selection. Glance through the selection quickly to see what other information you can pick up. Look for anything that will help you read fluently and with understanding. Are there names, dates, or numbers? If so, you may have to read more slowly.

Reading for Meaning

Here are some ways to make sure you are making sense of what you read.

Build your concentration. You cannot understand what you read if you are not concentrating. When you discover that your thoughts are straying, correct the situation right away. Avoid distractions and distracting situations. Keep in mind the information you learned from previewing. This will help focus your attention on the selection.

Read in thought groups. Try to see meaningful combinations of words—phrases, clauses, or sentences. If you look at only one word at a time (called word-by-word reading), both your comprehension and your reading speed suffer.

Ask yourself questions. To sustain the pace you have set for yourself and to maintain a high level of concentration and comprehension, ask yourself questions such as What does this mean? or How can I use this information? as you read.

Finding the Main Ideas

The paragraph is the basic unit of meaning. If you can quickly discover and understand the main idea of each paragraph, you will build your comprehension of the selection.

Find the topic sentence. The topic sentence, which contains the main idea, often is the first sentence of a paragraph. It is followed by sentences that support, develop, or explain the main idea. Sometimes a topic sentence comes at the end of a paragraph. When it does, the supporting details come first, building the base for the topic sentence. Some paragraphs do not have a topic sentence; all of the sentences combine to create a meaningful idea.

Understand paragraph structure. Every well-written paragraph has a purpose. The purpose may be to inform, define, explain or illustrate. The purpose should always relate to the main idea and expand on it. As you read each paragraph, see how the body of the paragraph tells you more about the main idea.

Relate ideas as you read. As you read the selection, notice how the writer puts together ideas. As you discover the relationship between the ideas, the main ideas come through quickly and clearly.

Mastering Reading Comprehension

Reading fast is not useful if you don't remember or understand what you read. The two exercises in Part A provide a check on how well you have understood the article.

Recalling Facts

These multiple-choice questions provide a quick check to see how well you recall important information from the article. As you learn to apply the reading strategies described earlier, you should be able to answer these questions more successfully.

Understanding Ideas

These questions require you to think about the main ideas in the article. Some main ideas are stated in the article; others are not. To answer some of the questions, you need to draw conclusions about what you read.

The five exercises in Part B require multiple answers. These exercises provide practice in applying comprehension and critical-thinking skills that you can use in all your reading.

Recognizing Words in Context

Always check to see whether the words around an unfamiliar word—its context—can give you a clue to the word's meaning. A word generally appears in a context related to its meaning.

Suppose, for example, that you are unsure of the meaning of the word *expired* in the following passage:

> Vera wanted to check out a book, but her library card had expired. She had to borrow my card, because she didn't have time to renew hers.

You could begin to figure out the meaning of *expired* by asking yourself a question such as, What could have happened to Vera's library card that would make her need to borrow someone else's card? You might realize that if Vera had to renew her card, its usefulness must have come to an end or run out. This would lead you to conclude that the word *expired* must mean "to come to an end" or "to run out." You would be right. The context suggested the meaning.

Context can also affect the meaning of a word you already know. The word *key,* for instance, has many meanings. There are musical keys, door keys, and keys to solving a mystery. The context in which the word *key* occurs will tell you which meaning is correct.

Sometimes a word is explained by the words that immediately follow it. The subject of a sentence and your knowledge about that subject might also help you determine the meaning of an unknown word. Try to decide the meaning of the word *revive* in the following sentence:

> Sunshine and water will revive those drooping plants.

The compound subject is *sunshine* and *water*. You know that plants need light and water to survive and that drooping plants are not healthy. You can figure out that *revive* means "to bring back to health."

Distinguishing Fact from Opinion

Every day you are called upon to sort out fact and opinion. Because much of what you read and hear contains both facts and opinions, you need to be able to tell the two apart.

Facts are statements that can be proved true. The proof must be objective and verifiable. You must be able to check for yourself to confirm a fact.

Look at the following facts. Notice that they can be checked for accuracy and confirmed. Suggested sources for verification appear in parentheses.

- Abraham Lincoln was the 16th president of the United States. (Consult biographies, social studies books, encyclopedias, and similar sources.)

- Earth revolves around the Sun. (Research in encyclopedias or astronomy books; ask knowledgeable people.)
- Dogs walk on four legs. (See for yourself.)

Opinions are statements that cannot be proved true. There is no objective evidence you can consult to check the truthfulness of an opinion. Unlike facts, opinions express personal beliefs or judgments. Opinions reveal how someone feels about a subject, not the facts about that subject. You might agree or disagree with someone's opinion, but you cannot prove it right or wrong.

Look at the following opinions. The reasons these statements are classified as opinions appear in parentheses.

- Abraham Lincoln was born to be a president. (You cannot prove this by referring to birth records. There is no evidence to support this belief.)
- Earth is the only planet in our solar system where intelligent life exists. (There is no proof of this. It may be proved true some day, but for now it is just an educated guess—not a fact.)
- The dog is a human's best friend. (This is not a fact; your best friend might not be a dog.)

As you read, be aware that facts and opinions are often mixed together. Both are useful to you as a reader. But to evaluate what you read and to read intelligently, you need to know the difference between the two.

Keeping Events in Order

Sequence, or chronological order, is the order of events in a story or article or the order of steps in a process. Paying attention to the sequence of events or steps will help you follow what is happening, predict what might happen next, and make sense of a passage.

To make the sequence as clear as possible, writers often use signal words to help the reader get a more exact idea of when things happen. Following is a list of frequently used signal words and phrases:

until	first
next	then
before	after
finally	later
when	while
during	now
at the end	by the time
as soon as	in the beginning

Signal words and phrases are also useful when a writer chooses to relate details or events out of sequence. You need to pay careful attention to determine the correct chronological order.

Making Correct Inferences

Much of what you read *suggests* more than it *says*. Writers often do not state ideas directly in a text. They can't. Think of the time and space it would take to state every idea. And think of how boring that would be! Instead, writers leave it to you, the reader, to fill in the information they leave out—to make inferences. You do this by combining clues in the story or article with knowledge from your own experience.

You make many inferences every day. Suppose, for example, that you are visiting a friend's house for the first time. You see a bag of kitty litter. You infer (make an inference) that the family has a cat. Another day you overhear a conversation. You catch the names of two actors and the words *scene, dialogue*, and *directing*. You infer that the people are discussing a movie or play.

In these situations and others like them, you infer unstated information from what you observe or read. Readers must make inferences in order to understand text.

Be careful about the inferences you make. One set of facts may suggest several inferences. Some of these inferences could be faulty. A correct inference must be supported by evidence.

Remember that bag of kitty litter that caused you to infer that your friend has a cat? That could be a faulty inference. Perhaps your friend's family uses the kitty litter on their icy sidewalks to create traction. To be sure your inference is correct, you need more evidence.

Understanding Main Ideas

The main idea is the most important idea in a paragraph or passage—the idea that provides purpose and direction. The rest of the selection explains, develops, or supports the main idea. Without a main idea, there would be only a collection of unconnected thoughts.

In the following paragraph, the main idea is printed in italics. As you read, observe how the other sentences develop or explain the main idea.

> *Typhoon Chris hit with full fury today on the central coast of Japan.* Heavy rain from the storm flooded the area. High waves carried many homes into the sea. People now fear that the heavy rains will cause mudslides in the central part of the country. The number of people killed by the storm may climb past the 200 mark by Saturday.

In this paragraph, the main-idea statement appears first. It is followed by sentences that explain, support, or give details. Sometimes the main idea appears at the end of a paragraph. Writers often put the main idea at the end of a paragraph when their purpose is to persuade or convince. Readers may be more open to a new idea if the reasons for it are presented first.

As you read the following paragraph, think about the overall impact of the supporting ideas. Their purpose is to convince the reader that the main idea in the last sentence should be accepted.

> Last week there was a head-on collision at Huntington and Canton streets. Just a month ago a pedestrian was struck there. Fortunately, she was only slightly injured. In the past year, there have been more accidents there than at any other corner in the city. In fact, nearly 10 percent of

> all accidents in the city occur at the corner. This intersection is very dangerous, and a traffic signal should be installed there before a life is lost.

The details in the paragraph progress from least important to most important. They achieve their full effect in the main idea statement at the end.

In many cases, the main idea is not expressed in a single sentence. The reader is called upon to interpret all of the ideas expressed in the paragraph and to decide upon a main idea. Read the following paragraph.

> The American author Jack London was once a pupil at the Cole Grammar School in Oakland, California. Each morning the class sang a song. When the teacher noticed that Jack wouldn't sing, she sent him to the principal. He returned to class with a note. The note said that Jack could be excused from singing with the class if he would write an essay every morning.

In this paragraph, the reader has to interpret the individual ideas and to decide on a main idea. This main idea seems reasonable: Jack London's career as a writer began with a punishment in grammar school.

Understanding the concept of the main idea and knowing how to find it is important. Transferring that understanding to your reading and study is also important.

Working Through a Lesson

Part A

1. **Preview the article.** Locate the timed selection in Part A of the lesson that you are going to read. Wait for your teacher's signal to preview. You will have 20 seconds for previewing. Follow the previewing steps described on page 2.

2. **Read the article.** When your teacher gives you the signal, begin reading. Read carefully so that you will be able to answer questions about what you have read. When you finish reading, look at the board and note your reading time. Write this time at the bottom of the page on the line labeled Reading Time.

3. **Complete the exercises.** Answer the 10 questions that follow the article. There are 5 fact questions and 5 idea questions. Choose the best answer to each question and put an X in that box.

4. **Correct your work.** Use the Answer Key at the back of the book to check your answers. Circle any wrong answer and put an X in the box you should have marked. Record the number of correct answers on the appropriate line at the end of the lesson.

Part B

1. **Preview and read the passage.** Use the same techniques you

used to read Part A. Think about what you are reading.

2. **Complete the exercises.** Instructions are given for answering each category of question. There are 15 responses for you to record.

3. **Correct your work.** Use the Answer Key at the back of the book. Circle any wrong answer and write the correct letter or number next to it. Record the number of correct answers on the appropriate line at the end of the lesson.

Plotting Your Progress

1. **Find your reading rate.** Turn to the Reading Rate graph on page 116. Put an X at the point where the vertical line that represents the lesson intersects your reading time, shown along the left-hand side. The right-hand side of the graph will reveal your words-per-minute reading speed.

2. **Find your comprehension score.** Add your scores for Part A and Part B to determine your total number of correct answers. Turn to the Comprehension Score graph on page 117. Put an X at the point where the vertical line that represents your lesson intersects your total correct answers, shown along the left-hand side. The right-hand side of the graph will show the percentage of questions you answered correctly.

3. **Complete the Comprehension Skills Profile.** Turn to page 118. Record your incorrect answers for the Part B exercises. The five Part B skills are listed along the bottom. There are five columns of boxes, one column for each question. For every incorrect answer, put an X in a box for that skill.

To get the most benefit from these lessons, you need to take charge of your own progress in improving your reading speed and comprehension. Studying these graphs will help you to see whether your reading rate is increasing and to determine what skills you need to work on. Your teacher will also review the graphs to check your progress.

To the Teacher

About the Series

Timed Readings Plus in Science includes 10 books at reading levels 4–13, with one book at each level. Book One contains material at a fourth-grade reading level; Book Two at a fifth-grade level, and so on. The readability level is determined by the Fry Readability Scale and is not to be confused with grade or age level. The books are designed for use with students at middle-school level and above.

The purposes of the series are as follows:

- to provide systematic, structured reading practice that helps students improve their reading rate and comprehension skills
- to give students practice in reading and understanding informational articles in the content area of science
- to give students experience in reading various text types—informational, expository, narrative, and prescriptive
- to prepare students for taking standardized tests that include timed reading passages in various content areas
- to provide materials with a wide range of reading levels so that students can continue to practice and improve their reading rate and comprehension skills

Because the books are designed for use with students at designated reading levels rather than in a particular grade, the science topics in this series are not correlated to any grade-level curriculum. Most standardized tests require students to read and comprehend science passages. This series provides an opportunity for students to become familiar with the particular requirements of reading science. For example, the vocabulary in a science article is important. Students need to know certain words in order to understand the concepts and the information.

Each book in the series contains 25 two-part lessons. Part A focuses on improving reading rate. This section of the lesson consists of a 400-word timed informational article on a science topic followed by two multiple-choice exercises. Recalling Facts includes five fact questions; Understanding Ideas includes five critical-thinking questions.

Part B concentrates on building mastery in critical areas of comprehension. This section consists of a nontimed passage—the “plus” passage—followed by five exercises that address five major comprehension skills. The passage varies in length; its subject matter relates to the content of the timed selection.

Timed Reading and Comprehension

Timed reading is the best-known method of improving reading speed. There is no point in someone's reading at an accelerated speed if the person does not understand what she or he is reading. Nothing is more important than comprehension in reading. The main purpose of reading is to gain knowledge and insight, to understand the information that the writer and the text are communicating.

Few students will be able to read a passage once and answer all of the questions correctly. A score of 70 or 80 percent correct is normal. If the student gets 90 or 100 percent correct, he or she is either reading too slowly or the material is at too low a reading level. A comprehension or critical thinking score of less than 70 percent indicates a need for improvement.

One method of improving comprehension and critical-thinking skills is for the student to go back and study each incorrect answer. First, the student should reread the question carefully. It is surprising how many students get the wrong answer simply because they have not read the question carefully. Then the student should look back in the passage to find the place where the question is answered, reread that part of the passage, and think about how to arrive at the correct answer. It is important to be able to recognize a correct answer when it is embedded in the text. Teacher guidance or class discussion will help the student find an answer.

Speed Versus Comprehension

It is not unusual for comprehension scores to decline as reading rate increases during the early weeks of timed readings. If this happens, students should attempt to level off their speed—but not lower it—and concentrate more on comprehension. Usually, if students maintain the higher speed and concentrate on comprehension, scores will gradually improve and within a week or two be back up to normal levels of 70 to 80 percent.

It is important to achieve a proper balance between speed and comprehension. An inefficient reader typically reads everything at one speed, usually slowly. Some poor readers, however, read rapidly but without satisfactory comprehension. It is important to achieve a balance between speed and comprehension. The practice that this series provides enables students to increase their reading speed while maintaining normal levels of comprehension.

Getting Started

As a rule, the passages in a book designed to improve reading speed should be relatively easy. The student should not have much difficulty with the vocabulary or the subject matter. Don't worry about the passages being too easy; students should see how quickly and efficiently they can read a passage.

Begin by assigning students to a level. A student should start with a book that is one level below his or her current reading level. If a student's reading level is not known, a suitable starting point would be one or two levels below the student's present grade in school.

Introduce students to the contents and format of the book they are using. Examine the book to see how it is organized. Talk about the parts of each lesson. Discuss the purpose of timed reading and the use of the progress graphs at the back of the book.

Timing the Reading

One suggestion for timing the reading is to have all students begin reading the selection at the same time. After one minute, write on the board the time that has elapsed and begin updating it at 10-second intervals (1:00, 1:10, 1:20, etc.). Another option is to have individual students time themselves with a stopwatch.

Teaching a Lesson

Part A

1. Give students the signal to begin previewing the lesson. Allow 20 seconds, then discuss special science terms or vocabulary that students found.
2. Use one of the methods described above to time students as they read the passage. (Include the 20-second preview time as part of the first minute.) Tell students to write down the last time shown on the board or the stopwatch when they finish reading. Have them record the time in the designated space after the passage.
3. Next, have students complete the exercises in Part A. Work with them to check their answers, using the Answer Key that begins on page 114. Have them circle incorrect answers, mark the correct answers, and then record the numbers of correct answers for Part A on the appropriate line at the end of the lesson. Correct responses to eight or more questions indicate satisfactory comprehension and recall.

Part B

1. Have students read the Part B passage and complete the exercises that follow it. Directions are provided with each exercise. Correct responses require deliberation and discrimination.
2. Work with students to check their answers. Then discuss the answers with them and have them record the number of correct answers for Part B at the end of the lesson.

Have students study the correct answers to the questions they answered incorrectly. It is important that they understand why a particular answer is correct or incorrect.

Have them reread relevant parts of a passage to clarify an answer. An effective cooperative activity is to have students work in pairs to discuss their answers, explain why they chose the answers they did, and try to resolve differences.

Monitoring Progress

Have students find their total correct answers for the lesson and record their reading time and scores on the graphs on pages 116 and 117. Then have them complete the Comprehension Skills Profile on page 118. For each incorrect response to a question in Part B, students should mark an X in the box above each question type.

The legend on the Reading Rate graph automatically converts reading times to words-per-minute rates. The Comprehension Score graph automatically converts the raw scores to percentages.

These graphs provide a visual record of a student's progress. This record gives the student and you an opportunity to evaluate the student's progress and to determine the types of exercises and skills he or she needs to concentrate on.

Diagnosis and Evaluation

The following are typical reading rates.

Slow Reader—150 Words Per Minute

Average Reader—250 Words Per Minute

Fast Reader—350 Words Per Minute

A student who consistently reads at an average or above-average rate (with satisfactory comprehension) is ready to advance to the next book in the series.

A column of Xs in the Comprehension Skills Profile indicates a specific comprehension weakness. Using the profile, you can assess trends in student performance and suggest remedial work if necessary.

1 A Flightless Birds

Most people think of birds as feathered animals that fly. Scientists, however, do not define birds as animals that fly, because some birds do not. Of the 10,000 or so species of birds, 46 cannot fly. Flight plays a key role in survival for most birds. It allows them to find food over a wide area and to get away from predators. Ancestors of flightless birds may have lost their ability to fly because they had no regular predators or did not need to fly to find food. Rather than fly, some of these birds developed other traits to catch food and avoid enemies. Two examples of flightless birds are penguins and ostriches.

Penguins are sea birds with flipperlike wings, dense feathers, and thick bodies. Unlike birds that fly, penguins do not have wide wings, large feathers, or hollow bones. In order to catch the fish they feed on, penguins use their powerful wings to swim swiftly. When they swim, they look as if they are flying through the water. Their torpedo-shaped bodies enable them to dive deep underwater, and their dense feathers protect them from the cold. Their swimming skill also helps them to escape from predators.

Ostriches, like emus and rheas, are members of a group of birds called ratites. These birds are known for their long legs, long necks, and large size. To protect themselves, ratites stay in groups and use their excellent vision and hearing to notice enemies. When danger approaches, these birds can run at speeds of more than 65 kilometers per hour (40 miles per hour) to escape. In addition to using their strong legs to run with, some ratites can deliver powerful kicks. The strong, heavy bones that enable these birds to run well also make them too heavy to fly.

Not all flightless birds have been successful at protecting themselves. Flightless birds on some islands had no enemies until people arrived. These birds were hunted and easily caught by people and the animals brought by people. Human land development has destroyed the habitats of some birds. A number of flightless birds—such as the dodo and the great auk—became extinct because they were unable to adapt to new conditions and new enemies. Today, the kakapo parrot and the takahe of New Zealand are near extinction as well. After millions of years of survival, these flightless birds have had their populations reduced to a few dozen.

Reading Time ______

Recalling Facts

1. Only 46 of the 10,000 or so species of birds do not
   - ❑ a. have feathers.
   - ❑ b. fly.
   - ❑ c. swim.
2. Flightless birds lost their ability to fly because
   - ❑ a. in the past they did not need it to survive.
   - ❑ b. they ate too much and became too heavy.
   - ❑ c. they could move faster by running.
3. Ratites are known for their
   - ❑ a. ability to swim swiftly.
   - ❑ b. keen sense of smell.
   - ❑ c. ability to run fast.
4. The purpose of a penguin's feathers is to
   - ❑ a. keep the penguin warm.
   - ❑ b. help the penguin fly.
   - ❑ c. help the penguin swim more swiftly.
5. The dodo and the great auk are two flightless birds that are
   - ❑ a. among the most common ratites.
   - ❑ b. endangered.
   - ❑ c. extinct.

Understanding Ideas

6. The article suggests that an accurate definition of a bird is
   - ❑ a. an animal that has lightweight bones and can fly.
   - ❑ b. an animal with wing structures and feathers.
   - ❑ c. an animal with claws that makes a nest.
7. The most likely reason that penguins do not fly is that
   - ❑ a. they are able to find their food by swimming.
   - ❑ b. there are no trees in their natural habitats.
   - ❑ c. the winds in Antarctica are very strong.
8. In contrast to the bodies of birds that fly, the bodies of flightless birds have
   - ❑ a. no wings.
   - ❑ b. heavier bones.
   - ❑ c. thinner feathers.
9. The article suggests that the greatest dangers to flightless island birds include
   - ❑ a. competition with other birds.
   - ❑ b. climate changes.
   - ❑ c. the arrival of new enemies.
10. One can infer that the areas where flightless birds have become extinct include
    - ❑ a. the United States.
    - ❑ b. North Africa.
    - ❑ c. islands in the Pacific Ocean.

1 B Wildlife Photography

Anyone who has tried to get close to an animal in the wild knows how difficult it can be. As a result, much of our knowledge of wildlife comes from pictures taken by skilled professionals that know how to approach these animals. These professionals are wildlife photographers.

Wildlife photographers rely not only on their photographic skills but also on their knowledge of wildlife. To get good pictures, they sometimes have to endure long waits, harsh weather, and even the threat of animal attacks.

Once they have become familiar with a location, photographers can begin to get close enough to animals to take pictures. Some photographers hide in hutlike structures called blinds. This technique works well with animals such as birds that depend mainly on their vision to sense danger. In contrast, blinds do not work well for taking pictures of animals with a keen sense of smell. Photographers may approach these animals on foot, staying downwind and avoiding sudden movements. Food or noises, such as birdcalls, may also be used to lure wildlife into view.

For difficult subjects, a photographer may even leave a camera in the wild with a trip line. Animals that touch the line trigger the camera to snap pictures of them. Each of these methods requires great patience and knowledge, but the reward can be a rare and fascinating glimpse of nature.

1. Recognizing Words in Context

Find the word *downwind* in the passage. One definition below is closest to the meaning of that word. One definition has the opposite or nearly opposite meaning. The remaining definition has a completely different meaning. Label the definitions C for *closest*, O for *opposite or nearly opposite*, and D for *different*.

______ a. in the direction the wind is coming from

______ b. in the direction the wind is blowing

______ c. perpendicular to the direction the wind is blowing

2. Distinguishing Fact from Opinion

Two of the statements below present *facts*, which can be proved correct. The other statement is an *opinion*, which expresses someone's thoughts or beliefs. Label the statements F for *fact* and O for *opinion*.

______ a. A wildlife photographer relies on photographic skills.

______ b. The best method for photographing wildlife is to approach on foot.

______ c. Sometimes photographers use food to attract wildlife.

3. Keeping Events in Order

Label the statements below 1, 2, and 3 to show the order in which the events happen.

_____ a. A wild animal touches the trip line of the camera.

_____ b. A photograph is taken of the animal.

_____ c. A photographer sets a camera in the wild with a trip line.

4. Making Correct Inferences

Two of the statements below are correct *inferences,* or reasonable guesses. They are based on information in the passage. The other statement is an incorrect, or faulty, inference. Label the statements C for *correct* inference and F for *faulty* inference.

_____ a. An impatient person would probably not make a good wildlife photographer.

_____ b. Many wildlife photographers use disposable cameras because they are easy to carry.

_____ c. A love of nature and wildlife is important for wildlife photographers.

5. Understanding Main Ideas

One of the statements below expresses the main idea of the passage. One statement is too general, or too broad. The other explains only part of the passage; it is too narrow. Label the statements M for *main idea,* B for *too broad,* and N for *too narrow.*

_____ a. Taking pictures of wildlife requires patience, knowledge, and skill.

_____ b. Photography is a powerful educational tool.

_____ c. Some wildlife photographers use structures called blinds.

Correct Answers, Part A _____

Correct Answers, Part B _____

Total Correct Answers _____

2 A Dressing for the Season

Like other mammals, humans are warm-blooded animals with standard body temperatures. The food that humans consume produces heat energy that keeps the body at about 37°C (98.6° F). Humans' stable body temperature, however, does not mean that humans are unaffected by heat or cold. In fact, prolonged exposure to extreme heat or cold can harm the body and even cause death.

One way to keep the body safe from heat or cold is to dress for the season. In areas with cold winters, people should wear thick, snug clothing. Snug clothing keeps the air that has been warmed by the body close to the skin. This reduces the loss of body heat. Winter hats are important, as about 40 percent of the heat that leaves the body leaves through the head. Being improperly dressed for the cold or staying out in the cold too long can lead to frostbite or hypothermia. Both of these conditions can be dangerous and may require medical treatment.

In the springtime, as the weather warms, lighter clothing can be worn. Nevertheless, spring in many areas brings wet conditions that can cause the body to lose heat. People should wear waterproof jackets to keep from getting wet during spring showers. When the body gets wet, water on the skin absorbs body heat. As the water evaporates, body heat is carried away and the body cools. Staying wet for too long can cause the body to lose heat continuously and get too cold. A chilled body is especially vulnerable to disease.

In the heat of summer, hats, sunglasses, and long clothing can protect the eyes and skin from the sun's harmful ultraviolet rays. To keep cool in the summer heat, it is best for people to wear light, loose clothing, because it allows cooler air to reach the body and carry warmer air away. To cool itself, the body may also begin to perspire. The sweat on the skin evaporates, carrying body heat away with it. If the body gets too hot, heat stroke can result.

As it begins to grow cool in the autumn, a fall breeze can cut through light clothing and chill the body by carrying away warm air near the skin and replacing it with cool air. Wearing a windbreaker or other light jacket can reduce this loss of heat. Being properly dressed for all seasons helps to keep the body comfortable and healthy.

Reading Time ______

Recalling Facts

1. The temperature 37° C represents
   - ❑ a. the standard human body temperature.
   - ❑ b. a dangerously high body temperature.
   - ❑ c. a dangerously low body temperature.

2. Hypothermia is a dangerous condition that results from
   - ❑ a. extreme heat.
   - ❑ b. extreme cold.
   - ❑ c. sunburn.

3. About ______ percent of the heat that leaves the body leaves through the head.
   - ❑ a. 70
   - ❑ b. 10
   - ❑ c. 40

4. Waterproof jackets are helpful because
   - ❑ a. they keep the body warm even on the coldest days.
   - ❑ b. water on the skin absorbs body heat.
   - ❑ c. they are the best way to protect the body from chilly breezes.

5. Perspiring cools the body because
   - ❑ a. sweat is a cool liquid.
   - ❑ b. sweat attracts cool air to the skin.
   - ❑ c. when sweat evaporates it takes body heat away with it.

Understanding Ideas

6. One can infer that one of the main reasons that people sometimes do not dress for the season is that
   - ❑ a. they believe they will never get sick.
   - ❑ b. sometimes the weather changes gradually and people do not notice.
   - ❑ c. people are not sure what kind of clothes they should wear in the winter.

7. It is most likely that misting water over the skin
   - ❑ a. would cool the body.
   - ❑ b. would warm the body.
   - ❑ c. would cause hypothermia.

8. One can infer that the meaning of the word *evaporate* has to do with
   - ❑ a. water changing to vapor and moving away through the air.
   - ❑ b. heat being absorbed into the skin.
   - ❑ c. snug clothing keeping warm air close to the skin.

9. It is likely that swimming in the summer cools the body because
   - ❑ a. water evaporates from the legs as a person is swimming.
   - ❑ b. the water temperature is lower than the body temperature.
   - ❑ c. swimming causes the body to perspire in the water.

10. What article of clothing would be helpful in avoiding both heat stroke and ultraviolet rays?
    - ❑ a. a light, loose-fitting, long-sleeved shirt
    - ❑ b. a short-sleeved T-shirt
    - ❑ c. a bathing suit

2 B Protection from the Sun

Ultraviolet rays, or UV rays, from the sun can harm the eyes and skin. In the short term, bright sunlight can cause eyestrain as the eyes struggle to focus through the glare of bright light. Too much sun in one day also can cause painful sunburn. In the long term, the sun's harmful ultraviolet rays can damage the sensitive retina at the back of the eye or cause cataracts. Long-term damaging effects to the skin include wrinkles, spots, growths, and skin cancer.

To protect the eyes from the sun's harmful UV rays, a person should wear sunglasses that carry a label certifying that they block UV rays. Materials in the lenses of these sunglasses absorb UV rays so that they do not enter and harm the eyes. Wearing a wide-brimmed hat will shade the eyes and protect skin on the head as well.

To protect skin on other parts of the body from UV rays, a person should wear long, loose clothing. The fabric should not be so loosely woven that it allows some sunlight to filter through. If the fabric is sheer and does not block sunlight, or if areas of skin are not covered, it is a good idea to wear sunscreen. Sunscreen alone is not enough, however, to prevent sun damage to the skin. A person must avoid spending long periods of time in the sun if at all possible.

1. Recognizing Words in Context

Find the word *sheer* in the passage. One definition below is closest to the meaning of that word. One definition has the opposite or nearly opposite meaning. The remaining definition has a completely different meaning. Label the definitions C for *closest,* O for *opposite or nearly opposite,* and D for *different.*

_____ a. short

_____ b. thin

_____ c. thick

2. Distinguishing Fact from Opinion

Two of the statements below present *facts,* which can be proved correct. The other statement is an *opinion,* which expresses someone's thoughts or beliefs. Label the statements F for *fact* and O for *opinion.*

_____ a. Special sunglasses protect the eyes from UV rays.

_____ b. The right clothing can protect the skin from harmful rays of the sun.

_____ c. Sunscreen provides the best protection from the sun.

3. Keeping Events in Order

Two of the statements below describe events that happened at the same time. The other statement describes an event that happened before or after those events. Label them S for *same time*, B for *before*, or A for *after*.

______ a. A person does not wear sunglasses.

______ b. The risk of retina damage, cataracts, and skin cancer increases.

______ c. A person spends many hours in the sun.

4. Making Correct Inferences

Two of the statements below are correct *inferences*, or reasonable guesses. They are based on information in the passage. The other statement is an incorrect, or faulty, inference. Label the statements C for *correct* inference and F for *faulty* inference.

______ a. It is a good idea to stay out of the sun at all times.

______ b. Sunscreen offers only limited protection if a person spends all day outside.

______ c. By the time a person realizes the sun has caused health problems, it may be too late to do much about it.

5. Understanding Main Ideas

One of the statements below expresses the main idea of the passage. One statement is too general, or too broad. The other explains only part of the passage; it is too narrow. Label the statements M for *main idea*, B for *too broad*, and N for *too narrow*.

______ a. Proper clothing and sunscreen can help prevent skin cancer.

______ b. The sun's harmful UV rays have damaging effects on the living things on Earth.

______ c. Protecting the skin and eyes from the sun's harmful rays can prevent short-term and long-term health problems.

Correct Answers, Part A ______

Correct Answers, Part B ______

Total Correct Answers ______

3 A Home Entertainment

Most homes in the United States have several machines that provide entertainment. Over the last 150 years, four machines in particular have played major roles in the development of home entertainment as we know it today. These machines are the phonograph, the radio, the television set, and the home computer.

In 1877, Thomas Edison became the first person to record and play back the human voice. He did this with one of his most popular inventions—the phonograph. In his design, Edison used parts from two other machines: the needle from the telegraph and the mouthpiece from the telephone. Edison's phonograph was different from later phonographs, also called record players. Instead of playing sounds recorded on a disk-shaped record, it played sounds recorded on a cylinder covered with tinfoil.

In the late 1880s, phonographs were offered for sale to the public. For the first time, people could hear recorded music in their homes. The phonograph remained popular until cassette tapes and compact discs appeared on the scene.

Guglielmo Marconi of Italy invented the radio in 1896. Radio broadcasts became popular in the 1920s, and people were able to bring entertainment into their living rooms without buying phonograph records.

The ideas that led to modern television came about through years of work by many inventors. Two Americans are usually credited with inventing the television set. Philo Farnsworth and Vladimir Zworykin designed some of the first sets in the late 1920s. Television broadcasts in the United States began in 1939. In 1945, there were only about 10,000 television sets in the country. By 1953, half of the homes in the United States had television sets.

Although the first computer actually was designed in 1936 for use by scientists to perform mathematical calculations, computers for personal use were created much later. The first home computers were sold as kits. The buyer used the kit to build the computer. Among the first home computer kits were the Scelbi and the Mark-8, both of which became available in 1974. These early units had little memory for programming, and there was no software. Users had to write their own software.

There have been many advances in home computers since these first models. Today, their entertainment uses include playing games and listening to music on compact discs. Like the phonograph, the radio, and the television set before it, the computer is shaping modern home entertainment.

Reading Time ______

Recalling Facts

1. The first device invented to record and play back the human voice was
   - ❑ a. the cassette recorder.
   - ❑ b. the computer.
   - ❑ c. the phonograph.

2. Guglielmo Marconi invented the
   - ❑ a. radio.
   - ❑ b. phonograph.
   - ❑ c. home computer.

3. Television sets became common in U.S. homes in the
   - ❑ a. 1930s.
   - ❑ b. 1950s.
   - ❑ c. 1970s.

4. The first home computers were sold in 1974 as
   - ❑ a. build-it-yourself kits.
   - ❑ b. television sets.
   - ❑ c. home stereo systems.

5. A home entertainment device that has been replaced by other devices is the
   - ❑ a. home computer.
   - ❑ b. radio.
   - ❑ c. phonograph.

Understanding Ideas

6. One can infer that many forms of home entertainment involve
   - ❑ a. computer games.
   - ❑ b. movies.
   - ❑ c. music.

7. One can infer that the owners of the first home computers needed to
   - ❑ a. work for the companies that sold the computers.
   - ❑ b. have college degrees.
   - ❑ c. have technical skills involving computers.

8. One can conclude from the article that modern home entertainment is possible due mainly to
   - ❑ a. inventions that allowed sound to be stored and transmitted.
   - ❑ b. telephone communications.
   - ❑ c. the invention of the calculator.

9. An important way that entertainment on a home computer is different from entertainment on other devices is that
   - ❑ a. more people use home computers than other devices.
   - ❑ b. the sound quality is better on home computers than it is on other devices.
   - ❑ c. most computer programs are designed for one or two people to use at a time.

10. From the article, it can be assumed that a new invention
    - ❑ a. often relies on ideas from earlier inventions.
    - ❑ b. always becomes widely used within a few years.
    - ❑ c. is based entirely on the work of one person.

3 | B

Home Audio: From Tinfoil to Compact Discs

The phonograph designed by Thomas Edison in 1877 was the first device to record and play back the human voice. The tinfoil cylinder that held the recorded sounds, however, could be played back only once. The gramophone designed by Emile Berliner in 1887 improved Edison's machine. It used flat disks, called records, that were mass produced and could be played again and again.

When the first radio programs were broadcast in the 1920s, people wondered if record sales would end. Some thought that radio programs might end the need for other home audio machines. Record sales did drop for a short time but then recovered and remained high until the 1980s.

Other forms of home audio materials became popular in the second half of the 20th century. Cassette tapes that used reels of magnetic tape to record and replay sound were first sold in the United States in 1964. In the late 1960s, James T. Russell developed the compact disc. This disc does not need to be touched by machine parts to be recorded or replayed. Instead, a laser beam reads the information from the disc. This makes the discs more durable than records or tapes. Compact discs can also store much more information than records or tapes can. By 1988 sales of compact discs were greater than those of records. Eventually most music companies stopped making records altogether.

1. Recognizing Words in Context

Find the word *durable* in the passage. One definition below is closest to the meaning of that word. One definition has the opposite or nearly opposite meaning. The remaining definition has a completely different meaning. Label the definitions C for *closest,* O for *opposite or nearly opposite,* and D for *different.*

______ a. quickly worn out

______ b. beneficial

______ c. long-lasting

2. Distinguishing Fact from Opinion

Two of the statements below present *facts,* which can be proved correct. The other statement is an *opinion,* which expresses someone's thoughts or beliefs. Label the statements F for *fact* and O for *opinion.*

______ a. The best way to listen to music is on compact disc.

______ b. Gramophone records could be played more than once.

______ c. Cassette tapes became popular after 1964.

3. Keeping Events in Order

Label the statements below 1, 2, and 3 to show the order in which the events happened.

_____ a. Radio broadcasts began.

_____ b. The compact disc virtually ended a century of record sales.

_____ c. The gramophone was invented.

4. Making Correct Inferences

Two of the statements below are correct *inferences,* or reasonable guesses. They are based on information in the passage. The other statement is an incorrect, or faulty, inference. Label the statements C for *correct* inference and F for *faulty* inference.

_____ a. Inventions are often improved upon.

_____ b. The compact disc has been replaced by a new invention.

_____ c. Most compact discs have better sound quality than records do.

5. Understanding Main Ideas

One of the statements below expresses the main idea of the passage. One statement is too general, or too broad. The other explains only part of the passage; it is too narrow. Label the statements M for *main idea,* B for *too broad,* and N for *too narrow.*

_____ a. Emile Berliner invented the gramophone.

_____ b. Music can be recorded and played back in a variety of ways.

_____ c. Home audio devices have changed and improved over time.

Correct Answers, Part A _____

Correct Answers, Part B _____

Total Correct Answers _____

4 A Research on the Internet

Suppose a student on the West Coast were doing a research project on a recent hurricane on the East Coast. Finding good sources from far away might be difficult. Library periodicals might offer some general facts. But finding more detailed sources could be very difficult—unless the student used the Internet. With the use of the Internet, a person has access to billions of pieces of information. Local newspapers, weather data, and government figures are just some of the sources the Internet makes available.

The Internet is a powerful research tool that links computers around the world. It provides a quick, low-cost way for people to share data. Once a computer links to the Internet, it can access data files throughout the network. But in order to read the wealth of data and graphics found on the part of the Internet called the World Wide Web, a computer user needs a program called a Web browser. World Wide Web files are called Web pages, and a group of these pages make up a Web site. Each Web page has a unique address called a URL, or uniform resource locator. Finding these information sources is usually easy if one uses a program called a search engine.

A search engine is a program on the Web that locates sites by searching for particular words, or keywords. When a person types in a keyword, the search engine lists links to Web pages that are related to the word. To access a Web page, the user simply clicks on a link in the list. The links use URLs to find the Web pages.

It is a good idea to check several of the links that come up in a search to find out which sites are best. Web sites operated by reliable institutions, such as universities and government agencies, are usually the best sources. Because of the Internet's open access, Web sites do exist that present inaccurate, and sometimes even offensive, information. That is why it is vital to assess the reliability of the site. Some Web sites focus more on opinions than on facts.

Sometimes a search does not provide the data needed. Advanced searches using other, related words—or different combinations of words—may bring up helpful Web pages. It is also a good idea to try more than one search engine when doing research, as each may provide different links.

Reading Time ______

Recalling Facts

1. The Internet
   - ❑ a. was invented in the years just before the start of the 20th century.
   - ❑ b. links computers around the world.
   - ❑ c. must be accessed by connecting with a library computer.

2. The World Wide Web is
   - ❑ a. part of the Internet.
   - ❑ b. a directory of keywords.
   - ❑ c. a graphics program.

3. A unique address used to connect to an individual Web page is a
   - ❑ a. browser.
   - ❑ b. search engine.
   - ❑ c. URL.

4. A program on the Web that uses keywords to locate sites is
   - ❑ a. an audio system.
   - ❑ b. a uniform resource locator.
   - ❑ c. a search engine.

5. As a research tool, the Internet provides
   - ❑ a. quick access to a large amount of data.
   - ❑ b. a slow, expensive way to do research.
   - ❑ c. few useful sources.

Understanding Ideas

6. One can conclude from the article that one of the main benefits of the Internet is
   - ❑ a. increased accuracy of data.
   - ❑ b. wider access to data.
   - ❑ c. inexpensive access to educational videos.

7. One can infer that Web pages are written
   - ❑ a. in many languages.
   - ❑ b. only in English.
   - ❑ c. only in European languages.

8. The article suggests that search engines allow searches to be performed
   - ❑ a. with keywords of fewer than ten letters.
   - ❑ b. in different ways.
   - ❑ c. by typing in the correct URL.

9. One can conclude from the article that the author
   - ❑ a. believes that the Internet has more drawbacks than benefits.
   - ❑ b. thinks that information on the Web will become more accurate over time.
   - ❑ c. is generally positive about the value of the Internet for research.

10. The article suggests that the best way to judge the reliability of a Web site is to determine
    - ❑ a. how many people use the site.
    - ❑ b. how many organizations have filed complaints about the site.
    - ❑ c. who operates the site.

4 B Writing a Science Research Paper

Writing a science research paper is an opportunity to explore a topic in depth. It involves gathering data for the chosen topic, organizing and supporting ideas, and identifying the sources used. Completing a well-documented paper with clear ideas can take many weeks of research and writing. Following the steps below can help a person write a strong, well-organized paper.

Step One: Start by finding general sources about the chosen topic. Reference books, periodicals, and the Internet are good places to start. A reference librarian can help you locate and use these sources. Your initial research should lead you to more detailed sources.

Step Two: When reading through the sources, take notes and keep track of which source each piece of information comes from. One way to do this is to list and number the sources on a sheet of paper. Write the number of the source alongside each note. This system makes it easy to list sources in footnotes and a bibliography.

Step Three: Organize your ideas before writing. A common structure includes an introduction with a main idea, supporting points, and a conclusion. To begin, write a paragraph that states the topic and main idea. Then present supporting points in the body of the paper. To finish the paper, write a concluding paragraph that reviews your most important points.

Step Four: List your sources in footnotes or a bibliography.

1. Recognizing Words in Context

Find the word *initial* in the passage. One definition below is closest to the meaning of that word. One definition has the opposite or nearly opposite meaning. The remaining definition has a completely different meaning. Label the definitions C for *closest,* O for *opposite or nearly opposite,* and D for *different.*

______ a. first

______ b. accurate

______ c. last

2. Distinguishing Fact from Opinion

Two of the statements below present *facts,* which can be proved correct. The other statement is an *opinion,* which expresses someone's thoughts or beliefs. Label the statements F for *fact* and O for *opinion.*

______ a. A bibliography is a list of sources.

______ b. A research paper takes time to complete.

______ c. Finding good sources is hard work.

3. Keeping Events in Order

Label the statements below 1, 2, and 3 to show the order in which the steps should be performed.

_____ a. Locate several sources.

_____ b. Begin writing the paper with an introduction.

_____ c. Organize ideas for the paper.

4. Making Correct Inferences

Two of the statements below are correct *inferences,* or reasonable guesses. They are based on information in the passage. The other statement is an incorrect, or faulty, inference. Label the statements C for *correct* inference and F for *faulty* inference.

_____ a. When writing a research paper, the research and the writing are both important.

_____ b. Every research paper should have a main idea.

_____ c. It is acceptable to begin writing a research paper after reading two sources.

5. Understanding Main Ideas

One of the statements below expresses the main idea of the passage. One statement is too general, or too broad. The other explains only part of the passage; it is too narrow. Label the statements M for *main idea,* B for *too broad,* and N for *too narrow.*

_____ a. Doing a science research paper requires gathering data and presenting ideas in writing.

_____ b. A reference librarian can help a student find sources for a research paper.

_____ c. Science projects include experiments, demonstrations, and research papers.

Correct Answers, Part A _____

Correct Answers, Part B _____

Total Correct Answers _____

5 A Oceanographers at Work

Oceanographers use science and technology to study many aspects of the ocean. They study marine plants and animals, the chemistry of the sea, the rocky ocean floor, and how the ocean interacts with the rest of the environment.

Oceanographers may work in the water, on land, or in both places. Some gather data and samples from the sea by means of ships and special submarines. The research continues in land-based laboratories and offices, where oceanographers can analyze the information and mateial in greater detail.

One type of oceanographer—the marine biologist—looks at sea life. These life forms range from large animals such as whales to single-celled organisms visible only with microscopes. Lauren Mullineaux is a marine biologist who studies creatures that live on the ocean floor, which are called benthic animals. She looks at the larvae of tube worms, shellfish, and snails. Mullineaux collects samples of these young animals from the ocean depths by means of a research submarine. Oceanographer Melanie Summit collects her samples of microbes from hot vents in the sea floor in the same way. The vents release heat from molten rock beneath the sea floor. These organisms can live without light or oxygen, and they may provide clues about how life on Earth began.

Another type of oceanographer is the chemical oceanographer. Chemical oceanographers study the chemical makeup of seawater. Some look for oil and natural gas deposits under the sea floor by analyzing seawater from various locations. Al Kaltenback has done this type of work for many years. Other chemical oceanographers look at ocean water to learn how pollution affects it.

Marine geologists, who are also oceanographers, study the minerals and rocks of the ocean floor. Wen-Lu Zhu examines rocks from beneath the surface of the ocean floor to learn about Earth's crust and how it formed. Dawn Wright studies how cracks on the ocean floor form hot vents. Wright's work also includes mapping the oceans.

A fourth type of oceanographer studies physical aspects of the sea, such as tides, currents, and temperature. Researchers in physical oceanography often search for links between the ocean and the weather. Kathryn Kelly studies the ocean without leaving her office. She examines satellite images and data on her computer to learn how the ocean affects climate. Although nowhere near the water, Kelly is not unlike other oceanographers. She uses science and technology to study the ocean and find clues about Earth.

Reading Time ______

Recalling Facts

1. A scientist who studies the ocean is called
   - ❑ a. a geologist.
   - ❑ b. a biologist.
   - ❑ c. an oceanographer.

2. A marine biologist studies
   - ❑ a. life forms in the ocean.
   - ❑ b. rocks on the ocean floor.
   - ❑ c. how weather affects the ocean.

3. A kind of oceanographer who studies rocks on the sea floor is a
   - ❑ a. chemical oceanographer.
   - ❑ b. marine geologist.
   - ❑ c. marine zoologist.

4. A physical oceanographer studies tides, currents, and temperature to understand the link between
   - ❑ a. the ocean and the climate.
   - ❑ b. the ocean and the shore.
   - ❑ c. forests and the weather.

5. Tiny organisms found near hot vents in the ocean floor may provide clues about
   - ❑ a. the first life forms on Earth.
   - ❑ b. the causes of diseases in fish.
   - ❑ c. the sources of water pollution.

Understanding Ideas

6. One can conclude from the article that technology is used
   - ❑ a. mostly by geologists studying rock formations.
   - ❑ b. mostly when scientists conduct research in submarines.
   - ❑ c. in all branches of oceanography.

7. The effects of an oil spill on marine life would probably be studied by
   - ❑ a. a geologist and a marine biologist.
   - ❑ b. a marine biologist and a chemical oceanographer.
   - ❑ c. a meteorologist and a chemical oceanographer.

8. Compared with a chemical oceanographer, an oceanographer who studies weather and climate
   - ❑ a. is less likely to rely on satellite technology.
   - ❑ b. is more likely to study seawater.
   - ❑ c. is less likely to work on a boat.

9. One can conclude that oceanographers study the ocean to learn about
   - ❑ a. Earth's origins, life, and resources.
   - ❑ b. early human cultures.
   - ❑ c. medicinal microbes.

10. It is likely that oceanographers who specialize in one branch of science
    - ❑ a. work separately from other oceanographers.
    - ❑ b. work only with oceanographers from the same branch of science.
    - ❑ c. exchange information with other kinds of scientists.

5 B The JASON Project

In 1985, oceanographer Robert D. Ballard and his crew discovered the wreck of the *Titanic* on the ocean floor. Ballard received many letters from students after he found the famous ship. They wanted to know how they could explore the ocean as he had. As a result, Ballard established the JASON Project, named after the ancient Greek hero Jason.

In Greek mythology, the young explorer Jason and his team of sailors set off on a quest to unknown lands and seas. On their journey, they face challenging and exciting adventures before achieving their goal. This story mirrors Ballard's concept for the JASON Project in many ways. The JASON Project sends students on an exciting mission through the sciences.

The JASON Project is a program for fourth- through ninth-graders and their teachers. The goal of the program is to inspire students to pursue the study of science. Each year students and their teachers explore a new adventure with the project. They use articles, videos, the Internet, and live broadcasts to learn about a topic. Project topics have included the land and peoples of the Hawaiian Islands, the rain forests, and the ocean. Through their journeys with the JASON Project, students experience adventures in science and learning.

1. Recognizing Words in Context

Find the word *established* in the passage. One definition below is closest to the meaning of that word. One definition has the opposite or nearly opposite meaning. The remaining definition has a completely different meaning. Label the definitions C for *closest,* O for *opposite or nearly opposite,* and D for *different.*

_____ a. created

_____ b. ended

_____ c. studied

2. Distinguishing Fact from Opinion

Two of the statements below present *facts,* which can be proved correct. The other statement is an *opinion,* which expresses someone's thoughts or beliefs. Label the statements F for *fact* and O for *opinion.*

_____ a. The JASON Project is named after a Greek hero.

_____ b. Robert D. Ballard is an oceanographer.

_____ c. The success of the JASON Project is an important accomplishment.

3. Keeping Events in Order

Two of the statements below describe events that happen at the same time. The other statement describes an event that happens before or after those events. Label them S for *same time,* B for *before,* or A for *after.*

______ a. Robert D. Ballard founds a program to inspire students in the sciences.

______ b. Robert D. Ballard and his crew discover the wreck of the *Titanic.*

______ c. Robert D. Ballard names the project after a mythic Greek sailor.

4. Making Correct Inferences

Two of the statements below are correct *inferences,* or reasonable guesses. They are based on information in the passage. The other statement is an incorrect, or faulty, inference. Label the statements C for *correct* inference and F for *faulty* inference.

______ a. The JASON Project requires students to take trips to learn about a topic.

______ b. The mission of the JASON Project is to inspire students in the sciences.

______ c. Robert Ballard is interested in helping young people.

5. Understanding Main Ideas

One of the statements below expresses the main idea of the passage. One statement is too general, or too broad. The other explains only part of the passage; it is too narrow. Label the statements M for *main idea,* B for *too broad,* and N for *too narrow.*

______ a. Jason is a character from Greek mythology.

______ b. Robert D. Ballard founded the JASON Project to inspire students in the sciences.

______ c. There are a number of programs for students interested in becoming scientists.

Correct Answers, Part A ______

Correct Answers, Part B ______

Total Correct Answers ______

6 A Muscles and Their Functions

The human body has three kinds of muscles: skeletal, smooth, and cardiac. Some muscles are always at work, even when the body is not moving. All three varieties of muscles do work by contracting, or becoming shorter. Muscles are involved in complex body functions, often without the person's being aware of them.

Skeletal muscles are attached to bones. Most of the muscle in the human body is skeletal muscle. Skeletal muscles support the body and cause it to move. These muscles have a striped appearance because they consist of interconnected strands of muscle fibers. Skeletal muscles are called voluntary muscles because they are controlled by parts of the brain that make decisions. An arm muscle will not bend the arm unless the brain sends a signal through a nerve. The nerve signal causes the muscle to contract. As the muscle shortens, it pulls on cords of tough tissue called tendons that are attached to a bone in the arm. The tendons pull on the bone, making the arm bend. To straighten the arm, the brain sends another message, causing a different muscle to contract. This second muscle pulls the bone in the other direction, causing the arm to straighten.

Once the body is asleep, skeletal muscles relax. This is why people sometimes unconsciously nod their heads when they fall asleep while sitting up. Skeletal muscles must remain contracted to support the neck. When these muscles relax, the head nods.

Smooth muscles line the insides of hollow organs. They enable these organs to perform many essential body functions, such as digesting food. These muscles can also be found in the walls of blood vessels and under the skin. Smooth muscles contract more slowly than skeletal muscles, but smooth-muscle contractions are more forceful. Smooth muscles receive messages to contract from nerves in the autonomic, or automatic, nervous system. This part of the nervous system consists of parts of the brain, including the brain stem, that operate automatically without conscious control.

Cardiac muscles are found only in the heart. Cardiac muscles allow the heart to beat in a steady rhythm in order to pump blood continuously through the body. Cardiac muscles receive messages to contract from a small section of the heart, called a node. The autonomic nervous system controls the rate at which cardiac muscles contract. As they contract, they squeeze the walls of the heart inward. This automatic action pumps blood to all parts of the body.

Reading Time ______

Recalling Facts

1. Skeletal muscles
   - ❑ a. are connected to bones.
   - ❑ b. work without a person's being aware of them.
   - ❑ c. are found mainly in organs and blood vessels.

2. The type of muscle that squeezes the walls of the heart to pump blood is
   - ❑ a. smooth muscle.
   - ❑ b. skeletal muscle.
   - ❑ c. cardiac muscle.

3. ______ support the structure of the body.
   - ❑ a. Skeletal muscles
   - ❑ b. Cardiac muscles
   - ❑ c. Involuntary muscles

4. Muscles that function without human awareness are called
   - ❑ a. dormant muscles.
   - ❑ b. involuntary muscles.
   - ❑ c. lazy muscles.

5. When a muscle shortens to cause movement or aid a body function, it is said to
   - ❑ a. relax.
   - ❑ b. extend.
   - ❑ c. contract.

Understanding Ideas

6. One can infer that the muscle that lines the intestines is
   - ❑ a. skeletal muscle.
   - ❑ b. smooth muscle.
   - ❑ c. cardiac muscle.

7. It is likely that muscles that support the spine are
   - ❑ a. skeletal muscles.
   - ❑ b. smooth muscles.
   - ❑ c. cardiac muscles.

8. One can infer that the muscles involved in ______ are under the control of the autonomic nerve system.
   - ❑ a. walking
   - ❑ b. supporting the skeleton
   - ❑ c. essential body functions

9. If a person started to run, the cardiac muscles would most likely
   - ❑ a. stop contracting rhythmically.
   - ❑ b. function in the same way as skeletal muscles.
   - ❑ c. contract at a faster rate.

10. It is likely that when a person is awake and active,
    - ❑ a. all three types of muscles are working together.
    - ❑ b. smooth muscles are not contracting.
    - ❑ c. cardiac muscles are less important than skeletal muscles.

6 B Training to Be a Runner

Running, like other forms of exercise, helps the body in important ways. These include strengthening the muscles and improving the fitness of the heart. Whether the goal is to win a race or just make it to the finish line of a 10-kilometer run, every runner should follow some basic guidelines for good health.

To benefit from training, avoiding injury is crucial. To help prevent injury, a runner should do some light activity and stretching before a workout. Light activity such as walking will warm muscles, allowing them to contract more easily. Once muscles have warmed up, a person can do stretching exercises. After a workout, one can do more stretches to reduce muscle tightness. In addition to warm-ups and stretching, a pair of running shoes that properly support and cushion the feet can help to prevent injury.

Planning proper training routines can also help runners to benefit from their workouts. A training routine should improve performance without causing injury or fatigue. An inexperienced runner should start with slow, short runs and gradually work up to faster speeds and longer distances. A new runner might alternate between jogging and walking during a workout. For more experienced runners, a weekly routine can include easy and strenuous workouts as well as days off. At the first sign of injury, it is best to stop running. Continuing to run when injured can cause a more serious injury.

1. Recognizing Words in Context

Find the word *strenuous* in the passage. One definition below is closest to the meaning of that word. One definition has the opposite or nearly opposite meaning. The remaining definition has a completely different meaning. Label the definitions C for *closest,* O for *opposite or nearly opposite,* and D for *different.*

______ a. healthful and enjoyable

______ b. requiring little energy

______ c. requiring much energy

2. Distinguishing Fact from Opinion

Two of the statements below present *facts,* which can be proved correct. The other statement is an *opinion,* which expresses someone's thoughts or beliefs. Label the statements F for *fact* and O for *opinion.*

______ a. Running is the best form of exercise.

______ b. A good running routine strengthens muscles and benefits the heart.

______ c. Proper running shoes can help prevent injury.

3. Keeping Events in Order

Label the statements below 1, 2, and 3 to show the order in which the events happen.

_____ a. A runner stretches to help prevent injury during a run.

_____ b. A runner does light activity to warm up muscles.

_____ c. A runner sets out on a strenuous run.

4. Making Correct Inferences

Two of the statements below are correct *inferences,* or reasonable guesses. They are based on information in the passage. The other statement is an incorrect, or faulty, inference. Label the statements C for *correct* inference and F for *faulty* inference.

_____ a. Some inexperienced runners become injured because they do not gradually work up to longer runs.

_____ b. People who run regularly tend to be healthier than people who do not exercise.

_____ c. Most runners suffer a serious injury at some point.

5. Understanding Main Ideas

One of the statements below expresses the main idea of the passage. One statement is too general, or too broad. The other explains only part of the passage; it is too narrow. Label the statements M for *main idea,* B for *too broad,* and N for *too narrow.*

_____ a. A good running routine benefits the heart.

_____ b. Following some basic guidelines can help people get the most out of running.

_____ c. Exercise benefits the body.

Correct Answers, Part A _____

Correct Answers, Part B _____

Total Correct Answers _____

7 A

The Science of Musical Instruments

Music is a grouping of sounds to produce an artistic effect. Sound occurs because an object vibrates. The vibration produces a sound wave that moves through the air. The rate of the vibration sets the pitch of the sound. A faster vibration makes a higher pitch; a slower vibration makes a lower, deeper pitch. The rates of vibrations produced by musical instruments determine the range of pitches that each can play.

In string instruments, plucking, striking, or strumming a set of taut strings or wires causes the vibrations. The length, thickness, and tightness of a string determines its pitch. Musicians playing violins, violas, cellos, and basses create sounds in basically the same way. They move a horsehair bow over the strings, which often are made of nylon fibers wrapped with aluminum thread. The shorter strings of the violin and the viola produce faster vibrations and higher pitches. The longer strings of the cello and the bass produce slower vibrations and lower pitches. Guitar strings are usually plucked or strummed, not played with a bow. When playing any of these instruments, a musician produces different notes by pressing down on the strings. This makes the vibrating part of the string shorter and raises its pitch. Some instruments, such as the piano and the harp, have a different string for each note.

In wind instruments such as flutes, clarinets, and horns, vibrations occur when air is blown through tubes. The blowing causes the column of air within the tube to vibrate, producing a sound. The length of the column of air determines the pitch of the sound. For example, a tuba has a coiled tube that would stretch out about 3.7 meters (12 feet) if it were straightened. A tuba produces a much lower pitch than a flute, which has a much shorter tube. Most wind instruments have keys or holes that a musician presses or covers with the fingers. This action changes the length of the column of vibrating air and produces different notes.

Musicians create vibrations in percussion instruments by striking the surface of the instruments. A xylophone player uses mallets to strike wooden bars of different lengths. Longer bars produce lower pitches, and shorter bars produce higher pitches. In a drum, the pitch is determined by the thickness and tightness of the membrane that stretches across the drum. A tighter, thinner membrane produces a higher sound than a looser, thicker membrane.

Reading Time ______

Recalling Facts

1. Sound waves are produced by
   - ❑ a. rays.
   - ❑ b. vibrations.
   - ❑ c. reflections.
2. The highness or lowness of a sound is called
   - ❑ a. tone.
   - ❑ b. pitch.
   - ❑ c. mood.
3. In string instruments, the vibration is created by the action of the musician's
   - ❑ a. hands.
   - ❑ b. mouth.
   - ❑ c. feet.
4. The pitch produced by a string instrument is determined by
   - ❑ a. the strength of the musician.
   - ❑ b. what the instrument is made of.
   - ❑ c. the length, tightness, and thickness of the strings.
5. The pitch produced by a wind instrument is determined by
   - ❑ a. the material the instrument is made of.
   - ❑ b. how wide the instrument is.
   - ❑ c. the length of the column of vibrating air.

Understanding Ideas

6. From the information in the article, one can conclude that music differs from other types of sounds because
   - ❑ a. musical sounds are organized into groups and have specific pitches.
   - ❑ b. musical instruments produce sounds that are more pleasant than all other sounds.
   - ❑ c. human beings create music.
7. One can infer that human vocal cords create sound in a way that is most similar to
   - ❑ a. string instruments.
   - ❑ b. wind instruments.
   - ❑ c. percussion instruments.
8. One can infer that the membrane of a drum can be adjusted to change its pitch just as ______ can.
   - ❑ a. the bow for a string instrument
   - ❑ b. the strings on a string instrument
   - ❑ c. a bar on a xylophone
9. A piccolo is like a flute but shorter, so one can infer that it produces pitches that are ______ those of a flute.
   - ❑ a. lower than
   - ❑ b. higher than
   - ❑ c. identical to
10. One can conclude from the article that blowing over the opening of an empty bottle produces a sound because it causes
    - ❑ a. the sides of the bottle to vibrate.
    - ❑ b. the lip of the bottle to vibrate.
    - ❑ c. the column of air inside the bottle to vibrate.

7 B What Determines Perfect Pitch?

Perfect pitch is a characteristic that few people possess. When a person can produce or recognize the pitch of a sound without comparing it with a standard set of sounds, the person is said to have perfect pitch. Because perfect pitch is so rare, scholars have tried to determine how people acquire it. Is perfect pitch a trait that is passed from parents to their children? Does musical training increase a person's chances of having perfect pitch? Research about spoken languages is providing some insight into these and other questions about perfect pitch.

A study done by psychology professor Diana Deutsch revealed that speakers of tone languages have perfect pitch. Many of the languages of Africa and East Asia are tone languages. In a tone language, the pitch of the word helps determine its meaning. The same sound spoken at different pitches can have different meanings. In her study, Deutsch found that speakers of Vietnamese and Mandarin Chinese had perfect pitch when reading a list of words in these languages.

The results of Deutsch's study suggest that all humans have the potential for perfect pitch. Only one person tested in her study had had any musical training. It appears that one need not have knowledge of music to attain perfect pitch. The study suggests that perfect pitch results as a person connects pitch with the meaning of words in the early years of life. It also shows that heredity does not determine perfect pitch.

1. Recognizing Words in Context

Find the word *attain* in the passage. One definition below is closest to the meaning of that word. One definition has the opposite or nearly opposite meaning. The remaining definition has a completely different meaning. Label the definitions C for *closest,* O for *opposite or nearly opposite,* and D for *different.*

______ a. lose

______ b. pronounce

______ c. achieve

2. Distinguishing Fact from Opinion

Two of the statements below present *facts,* which can be proved correct. The other statement is an *opinion,* which expresses someone's thoughts or beliefs. Label the statements F for *fact* and O for *opinion.*

______ a. Perfect pitch is not an important characteristic.

______ b. A study showed that speakers of Vietnamese have perfect pitch.

______ c. A person can have perfect pitch without receiving musical training.

3. Keeping Events in Order

Label the statements below 1, 2, and 3 to show the order in which the events happen.

_____ a. A young Chinese child begins to use different pitches to express different meanings.

_____ b. A young Chinese child begins to speak Mandarin Chinese.

_____ c. A young Chinese child develops perfect pitch.

4. Making Correct Inferences

Two of the statements below are correct *inferences*, or reasonable guesses. They are based on information in the passage. The other statement is an incorrect, or faulty, inference. Label the statements C for *correct* inference and F for *faulty* inference.

_____ a. People can have perfect pitch even if their parents do not.

_____ b. Perfect pitch is not a helpful characteristic for musicians.

_____ c. Pitch has different roles in different languages.

5. Understanding Main Ideas

One of the statements below expresses the main idea of the passage. One statement is too general, or too broad. The other explains only part of the passage; it is too narrow. Label the statements M for *main idea*, B for *too broad*, and N for *too narrow*.

_____ a. Some people have special abilities that involve sound.

_____ b. Diana Deutsch has studied speakers of tone languages.

_____ c. A study found a connection between tone languages and perfect pitch.

Correct Answers, Part A _____

Correct Answers, Part B _____

Total Correct Answers _____

8 A Energy in Its Many Forms

Energy is everywhere. It can be seen as light, heard as sound, and felt as heat. Energy can take many forms, but it is usually assigned to one of two major categories. These are kinetic energy, which is the energy of motion, and potential energy, which is stored energy. An object in motion has kinetic energy and performs work because of its motion. In physics, work refers to the movement of any object. An object at rest may be able to do work in the future because of its position. A ball at rest at the top of a hill has potential energy because of its position. At any time, the ball could do work by rolling down the hill. It would then have kinetic energy.

Forms of kinetic energy include heat, light, electricity, and sound. Each of these forms of kinetic energy involves the movement of small particles or parts. Heat results from the movement of atoms or molecules. As the atoms or molecules move faster, they get hotter. Light results from the movement of charged particles in an atom. As these charged particles—called electrons—change position in an atom, they give off light energy. Electricity, like light, involves the movement of electrons but from atom to atom. This flow of electrons is called an electric current. Sound involves the movement of air particles when vibrations push against them, making sound waves.

Potential energy, on the other hand, can take the form of chemical energy and nuclear energy. Chemical and nuclear energy are forms of stored energy capable of work. Chemical energy is stored in the bonds between atoms. When these bonds are broken, a chemical reaction takes place and changes the stored energy into the energy of motion. A similar breakage takes place when nuclear energy is released. The difference is that the atom itself is broken down. In this case, the stored energy in the matter that makes up the atom becomes kinetic energy.

A law used to define energy states that it is never lost or gained; it only changes form. Electrical energy becomes light energy in a light bulb. Nuclear energy becomes heat energy in a nuclear reactor. The body breaks down chemical energy in food and changes it to a different kind of chemical energy that can move muscles. Energy, either potential or kinetic, is involved in every aspect of life.

Reading Time ______

Recalling Facts

1. Two main types of energy into which all forms of energy can be grouped are
   - ❑ a. kinetic energy and heat energy.
   - ❑ b. light energy and potential energy.
   - ❑ c. kinetic energy and potential energy.
2. Heat, light, and sound are forms of energy that involve
   - ❑ a. the movement of particles.
   - ❑ b. particles at rest.
   - ❑ c. the breaking of particles.
3. Charged particles that move from atom to atom to produce an electric current are called
   - ❑ a. molecules.
   - ❑ b. electrons.
   - ❑ c. energy units.
4. Chemical energy is stored in the bonds between
   - ❑ a. electrons.
   - ❑ b. atoms.
   - ❑ c. particle of light.
5. One law of energy states that energy is not
   - ❑ a. involved in work.
   - ❑ b. changed from one form to another.
   - ❑ c. lost or gained.

Understanding Ideas

6. A child on a sled at the top of a snow-covered hill is an example of
   - ❑ a. potential energy.
   - ❑ b. kinetic energy.
   - ❑ c. electrical energy.
7. When a person plugs in a portable heater and turns it on,
   - ❑ a. heat energy changes to electrical energy.
   - ❑ b. light energy changes to heat energy.
   - ❑ c. electrical energy changes to heat energy.
8. The article suggests that food is
   - ❑ a. a form of potential energy.
   - ❑ b. a form of light energy.
   - ❑ c. not a form of energy.
9. The article suggests that, unlike other types of energy, chemical and nuclear energy
   - ❑ a. can never become kinetic energy.
   - ❑ b. are not types of kinetic energy themselves.
   - ❑ c. involve a breakdown between atoms or within an atom.
10. One can infer that the movement of steam from a pipe in a power plant is an example of
    - ❑ a. stored energy.
    - ❑ b. kinetic energy.
    - ❑ c. nuclear energy.

8 | B

Geothermal Energy: A Renewable Resource

People in many parts of the world depend on a great deal of energy for life's daily tasks. Some of the resources people depend on most are limited resources. Fossil fuels, such as coal, oil, and natural gas, are being used much more quickly than new fuel can form. In an effort to conserve these limited fuels, some countries are relying more and more on renewable sources of energy. Renewable energy sources are sources that cannot be used up.

One renewable resource, geothermal energy, consists of heat energy from deep within Earth. Earth's core is so hot that heat is always moving toward the surface. In some regions, this heat nears the surface in the form of very hot water in underground pools.

To use geothermal energy, workers drill wells to bring steam and hot water to Earth's surface. The steam and hot water cause turbines in power plants to spin and generate electricity. Water brought to the surface in this process is always returned to the underground pools to be reheated and reused. Hot water from geothermal wells also is used to heat buildings.

Using geothermal energy has several benefits. Not only does it reduce the use of scarce fossil fuels, but it also reduces pollution. The burning of fossil fuels pollutes the air, but production of geothermal energy does not. Geothermal energy is referred to as a clean resource.

1. Recognizing Words in Context

Find the word *conserve* in the passage. One definition below is closest to the meaning of that word. One definition has the opposite or nearly opposite meaning. The remaining definition has a completely different meaning. Label the definitions C for *closest,* O for *opposite or nearly opposite,* and D for *different.*

______ a. warm

______ b. waste

______ c. save

2. Distinguishing Fact from Opinion

Two of the statements below present *facts,* which can be proved correct. The other statement is an *opinion,* which expresses someone's thoughts or beliefs. Label the statements F for *fact* and O for *opinion.*

______ a. A benefit of geothermal energy is that it reduces pollution.

______ b. Fossil fuels are the most valuable forms of energy.

______ c. Geothermal energy produces electricity.

3. Keeping Events in Order

Two of the statements below describe events that happen at the same time. The other statement describes an event that happens before or after those events. Label them S for *same time,* B for *before,* or A for *after.*

_____ a. Steam and hot water brought to the surface produce electricity.

_____ b. Wells are drilled in geothermal pools.

_____ c. Hot water piped from pools heats buildings.

4. Making Correct Inferences

Two of the statements below are correct *inferences,* or reasonable guesses. They are based on information in the passage. The other statement is an incorrect, or faulty, inference. Label the statements C for *correct* inference and F for *faulty* inference.

_____ a. Geothermal energy is not available in some regions.

_____ b. People will soon stop using fossil fuels.

_____ c. Areas near volcanoes can provide geothermal energy.

5. Understanding Main Ideas

One of the statements below expresses the main idea of the passage. One statement is too general, or too broad. The other explains only part of the passage; it is too narrow. Label the statements M for *main idea,* B for *too broad,* and N for *too narrow.*

_____ a. Geothermal energy is a renewable resource with some important benefits.

_____ b. Geothermal energy produces electricity in power plants.

_____ c. Renewable resources are forms of energy that cannot be used up.

Correct Answers, Part A _____

Correct Answers, Part B _____

Total Correct Answers _____

9 | A

How a Tornado Forms

A tornado, sometimes called a twister, is a spinning column of air that touches down on Earth's surface. The winds that form these funnel-shaped storms spin at between 65 and 520 kilometers per hour (40 and 323 miles per hour). The winds create a vacuum in the funnel that sucks up objects in the tornado's path. Powerful tornadoes can lift up buildings and twenty-ton trailer trucks and drop them hundreds of meters away. They can flatten entire neighborhoods as well.

Tornados form during thunderstorms under precise conditions of temperature, moisture, and wind speed. When a mass of cold air and a mass of warm air meet, they form an unstable system called a front. The cold air, which is heavier, slides under the warm air. On a warm day, a layer of warm, moist air may become trapped below the front. If this happens, pressure builds until the ground layer of warm, moist air bursts through the upper layers and creates a tall, dark cloud called a thunderhead. Winds on Earth's surface produce an updraft that pushes warm, moist air into the thunderhead. If the wind conditions are right, the rising air begins to spin.

A tornado becomes possible when this rising air begins to gyrate in what scientists call a mesocyclone. The mesocyclone acts as a vacuum, sucking in warm air near the ground and spinning it upward into the thunderhead. This system may spin for a few moments and then disappear, or it may form at its base a smaller column of faster-spinning air called a funnel cloud. If the funnel cloud touches the ground, it becomes a tornado.

The conditions that form a tornado determine its shape, size, and strength. A waterspout is a tornado that forms over water, sucking water and sea life into the sky. A multivortex tornado is a large tornado with smaller funnels inside it. Clusters of tornadoes can touch down at the same time. This is called an outbreak. As a tornado touches down, it can take on a number of shapes, ranging from funnels to hourglasses to wide, dark cylinders. Some tornadoes are less than 30 meters (100 feet) wide at their base. Others are more than 1.5 kilometers (0.9 mile) wide. The amount of destruction caused by a tornado depends largely on the speed of the winds inside it. The stronger the winds are, the more destructive a tornado is likely to be.

Reading Time ______

Recalling Facts

1. A thunderhead forms when warm air at Earth's surface
   - ❑ a. forms a funnel cloud.
   - ❑ b. pushes upward through layers of cold and warm air.
   - ❑ c. loses heat and moisture.
2. Warm air that rises in updrafts and begins to spin is called a
   - ❑ a. mesocyclone.
   - ❑ b. flash flood.
   - ❑ c. front.
3. When a mass of cold air meets a mass of warm air, the system they form is called a
   - ❑ a. hail storm.
   - ❑ b. front.
   - ❑ c. high-pressure system.
4. A small column of faster-twisting air at the base of a mesocyclone is called a tornado when it
   - ❑ a. reaches a high speed.
   - ❑ b. passes over water.
   - ❑ c. touches the ground.
5. The most important factors in the formation of a tornado include
   - ❑ a. temperature, moisture, and wind speed.
   - ❑ b. cloud color, wind speed, and soil type.
   - ❑ c. rainfall, temperature, and nearness to oceans.

Understanding Ideas

6. One can conclude from the article that tornadoes are most likely to form
   - ❑ a. in areas where thunderstorms are common.
   - ❑ b. in the windiest areas.
   - ❑ c. over the ocean or a large lake.
7. From the article, one could conclude that a tornado would most likely occur
   - ❑ a. on a dry, windy day.
   - ❑ b. in the middle of winter.
   - ❑ c. on a summer afternoon.
8. One can infer that one of the most basic requirements for a tornado to form is
   - ❑ a. cool breezes.
   - ❑ b. rain.
   - ❑ c. the merging of masses of warm air and cold air.
9. The article suggests that a tornado is often accompanied by
   - ❑ a. thick white clouds.
   - ❑ b. earthquakes.
   - ❑ c. lightning.
10. Compared with a tornado, a mesocyclone
    - ❑ a. causes more destruction.
    - ❑ b. spins more slowly.
    - ❑ c. is a smaller storm system.

9 B Making a Tornado Safety Plan

Tornadoes kill an average of 80 people a year in the United States. Although a tornado only touches down in the same place about once every 250 years, it is a good idea to have a safety plan ready in areas where tornadoes are common. Such a plan can save lives. Tornadoes are most common in parts of Oklahoma, Texas, Kansas, Nebraska, and Iowa.

Knowing where to go is a vital part of a good safety plan. During a tornado, the safest place to be is in a basement. An interior room or a closet away from outside walls and windows are also good places to take shelter. Because mobile homes and cars may be picked up by tornadoes, they are not safe places to stay. If you are in an unsafe place, move to a nearby house or building but only if the tornado is still a good distance away. Food, water, blankets, flashlights, and radios should be stored at shelter sites before the tornado season begins.

Another key part of a safety plan is to stay aware of weather conditions during tornado season. The National Weather Service broadcasts tornado watches and warnings based on conditions. A tornado watch means that a tornado is possible, and a tornado warning means that one is nearby. If broadcasts are not available, stay alert to weather changes. Hail, fast-rushing clouds, roaring winds, greenish-black skies, and falling debris can signal a tornado.

1. Recognizing Words in Context

Find the word *interior* in the passage. One definition below is closest to the meaning of that word. One definition has the opposite or nearly opposite meaning. The remaining definition has a completely different meaning. Label the definitions C for *closest,* O for *opposite or nearly opposite,* and D for *different.*

______ a. outer

______ b. inner

______ c. extra

2. Distinguishing Fact from Opinion

Two of the statements below present *facts,* which can be proved correct. The other statement is an *opinion,* which expresses someone's thoughts or beliefs. Label the statements F for *fact* and O for *opinion.*

______ a. The National Weather Service broadcasts tornado warnings.

______ b. People must educate themselves about tornadoes.

______ c. Mobile homes are not safe places during tornadoes.

3. Keeping Events in Order

Label the statements below 1, 2, and 3 to show the order in which the events should happen.

_____ a. A tornado warning is issued for the area.

_____ b. Food and water are stored in a shelter site.

_____ c. Residents seek shelter right away.

4. Making Correct Inferences

Two of the statements below are correct *inferences,* or reasonable guesses. They are based on information in the passage. The other statement is an incorrect, or faulty, inference. Label the statements C for *correct* inference and F for *faulty* inference.

_____ a. A tornado can cause no harm if people plan for safety.

_____ b. Checking weather forecasts at least once a day is a good safety policy.

_____ c. Tornadoes happen most often in the South and the Midwest.

5. Understanding Main Ideas

One of the statements below expresses the main idea of the passage. One statement is too general, or too broad. The other explains only part of the passage; it is too narrow. Label the statements M for *main idea,* B for *too broad,* and N for *too narrow.*

_____ a. The National Weather Service alerts the public about tornadoes through watches and warnings.

_____ b. A good safety plan can help keep people avoid injury when tornadoes strike.

_____ c. Safety planning helps save lives in natural disasters.

Correct Answers, Part A _____

Correct Answers, Part B _____

Total Correct Answers _____

10 A Dinosaur Parents and Their Young

Like modern birds, dinosaurs laid hard-shelled eggs to produce young. It was once believed that dinosaurs, like modern reptiles, abandoned their eggs and did not care for their young. Recent fossil evidence, however, suggests that some dinosaurs did care for their young, as birds and other animals do today.

In 1993 in the Gobi Desert in Mongolia, scientists came across the skeleton of a dinosaur lying on a nest of eggs. An embryo from inside one of the eggs proved to be the same kind of dinosaur as the dinosaur sitting on the nest—an oviraptor. It appeared that the adult was sitting on its nest to protect its eggs. This find dispelled a myth that began in 1923 with the finding of the first oviraptor fossil, also lying on a nest. At that time, scientists believed that the dinosaur was stealing the eggs rather than protecting them. As a result, it was named oviraptor, which means "egg thief." In recent years, scientists have found other fossils of these dinosaurs lying on nests. Each one had its arms folded back over the eggs, in a way similar to the way a hen holds its wings.

Even before the truth about oviraptors was known, evidence from the nest sites of some duckbill dinosaurs showed that they cared for their young. In Montana in the early 1980s, scientists found a group of dinosaur nests with fossilized baby bones. The fossils showed that the legs of the young, like the legs of baby birds, had not yet become hard, solid bone. As a result, the dinosaur babies would not have been able to walk well or find food. They would have needed adult care to survive. Another nest site containing more mature young was found fossilized in volcanic ash. This suggested that young duckbill dinosaurs did not leave the protection of their nests, even when in danger. It appears that adult duckbills cared for their babies in nests to give the babies a better chance to survive.

In addition to caring for young in nests, some types of dinosaurs may have formed family units. Tracks of the large sauropods show half-grown young walking with adults. In 1992 in Wyoming, a fossilized group of adult and young hypsilophodont dinosaurs was found huddled together in a burrow. There is still more to learn about dinosaur families, however, and scientists may never know the entire story of dinosaur parents and their young.

Reading Time ______

Recalling Facts

1. Like birds, dinosaurs produced young by
   - ❑ a. laying eggs.
   - ❑ b. giving birth.
   - ❑ c. planting seeds.

2. A dinosaur believed to sit on its eggs much like a hen was the
   - ❑ a. aptosaurus.
   - ❑ b. oviraptor.
   - ❑ c. tyrannosaurus.

3. The scientists who named the oviraptor believed it was
   - ❑ a. stealing eggs.
   - ❑ b. protecting eggs.
   - ❑ c. abandoning eggs.

4. Evidence at group nest sites suggests that baby duckbill dinosours
   - ❑ a. could take care of themselves.
   - ❑ b. did not hatch from eggs.
   - ❑ c. needed care to survive.

5. The idea that some dinosaurs may have formed family groups or herds is supported by
   - ❑ a. tracks of adult and young sauropods.
   - ❑ b. the number of eggs in a nest.
   - ❑ c. discoveries in Mongolia.

Understanding Ideas

6. The article suggests that some dinosaurs may have been less like reptiles and more like
   - ❑ a. people.
   - ❑ b. fish.
   - ❑ c. birds.

7. From the article, one can infer that dinosaur fossils can be found
   - ❑ a. mostly in Asia and Europe.
   - ❑ b. mostly in North America.
   - ❑ c. in many parts of the world.

8. One can conclude from the article that living in family groups
   - ❑ a. was a trait of all dinosaurs.
   - ❑ b. may have been a trait of some dinosaurs.
   - ❑ c. was not a trait of any dinosaurs.

9. The article suggests that the most accurate evidence of dinosaur behavior comes from
   - ❑ a. comparisons with living creatures.
   - ❑ b. fossils.
   - ❑ c. the study of reptiles.

10. It is likely that early scientists thought oviraptors were stealing rather than protecting eggs because they thought dinosaurs
    - ❑ a. abandoned their eggs like reptiles.
    - ❑ b. watched over their eggs like birds.
    - ❑ c. gave birth like mammals.

10 B Discovering Dinosaur Eggs

Until the 20th century, scientists did not know that dinosaurs laid eggs. For thousands of years people had been finding fossilized eggs and eggshells, but they did not know what these objects were. A find at one site in Mongolia suggests that people may even have worn these fossils as jewelry thousands of years ago.

In the 1850s, Jean-Jacques Pouech, a French priest who liked to look for fossils, found fragments that he described as pieces of a huge eggshell. The egg would have been about the size of a basketball. At the time, neither Pouech nor anyone else knew what kind of creature the eggshell could have contained. Some people thought that a giant bird had laid the eggs. More than 100 years later, scientists proved that the fossils came from dinosaur eggs.

It was not until 1923 that the discovery of the first complete fossils of dinosaur eggs was made. A group of explorers, led by scientist Roy Chapman Andrews, found two nests containing fossilized eggs in the Gobi Desert in Mongolia. The first nest held five small, rounded eggs, and the second nest held five longer, larger eggs. Both the rounded eggs and the elongated eggs were shown to be dinosaur eggs. With their discovery, Andrews and his group were able to prove that dinosaurs had in fact laid eggs.

1. Recognizing Words in Context

Find the word *elongated* in the passage. One definition below is closest to the meaning of that word. One definition has the opposite or nearly opposite meaning. The remaining definition has a completely different meaning. Label the definitions C for *closest,* O for *opposite or nearly opposite,* and D for *different.*

______ a. cracked

______ b. shortened

______ c. stretched out

2. Distinguishing Fact from Opinion

Two of the statements below present *facts,* which can be proved correct. The other statement is an *opinion,* which expresses someone's thoughts or beliefs. Label the statements F for *fact* and O for *opinion.*

______ a. Finding the first dinosaur eggs was a tremendous accomplishment.

______ b. Jean-Jacques Pouech did not know what kind of animal his eggshells came from.

______ c. Roy Chapman Andrews led an expedition to Mongolia.

3. Keeping Events in Order

Label the statements below 1, 2, and 3 to show the order in which the events happen.

_____ a. The first complete fossils of dinosaur eggs are discovered in Mongolia.

_____ b. Jean-Jacques Pouech finds fossils that look like pieces of eggshell.

_____ c. Scientists determine that the eggs found by Pouech are dinosaur eggs.

4. Making Correct Inferences

Two of the statements below are correct *inferences,* or reasonable guesses. They are based on information in the passage. The other statement is an incorrect, or faulty, inference. Label the statements C for *correct* inference and F for *faulty* inference.

_____ a. Jean-Jacques Pouech eventually found out that his fossils were dinosaur eggs.

_____ b. Scientists could not prove that dinosaurs laid eggs until they found fossilized eggs.

_____ c. People knew little about dinosaurs before the 20th century.

5. Understanding Main Ideas

One of the statements below expresses the main idea of the passage. One statement is too general, or too broad. The other explains only part of the passage; it is too narrow. Label the statements M for *main idea,* B for *too broad,* and N for *too narrow.*

_____ a. Scientists have made many important discoveries of dinosaur fossils.

_____ b. The Gobi Desert in Mongolia has yielded fossils of dinosaur eggs.

_____ c. During the 20th century, scientists proved that dinosaurs laid eggs.

Correct Answers, Part A _____

Correct Answers, Part B _____

Total Correct Answers _____

11 A The Usefulness of Mud

From ancient to modern times, people have relied on natural materials. Mud is one natural material that has been useful to people in many cultures. This is because of its widespread availability. Mud can be found anywhere there is water and soil. Earth's surface is made up wholly of water and rock. Soil forms through the erosion of rock, so mud is a substance available to people in almost every part of the world.

Adobe bricks are widely used as a building material in dry regions such as Egypt, northern Mexico, and the Southwestern United States. The ancient Egyptians built homes with adobe bricks made of mud from the Nile River. They mixed the mud with straw in molds and let it bake in the sun. Today, people are still building homes with similar types of adobe bricks. Builders in the Southwest use adobe bricks even in modern structures, for decoration. Although some adobe bricks are still sun-dried in the traditional manner, businesses sell mud bricks that are heated, or fired, at high temperatures in an oven called a kiln.

The ancient Romans used fired clay to construct pipes to transport water and sewage. Clay, like sand and silt, is found in soil. When mixed with water, the fine texture of clay creates a smooth mud that is easy to shape. Clay heated at a high temperature is very sturdy.

In many parts of the world, people still produce clay-based pottery. Pueblo Indians, for instance, dig clay from the ground to use for pottery. They grind up the clay and mix it with water and other materials. Then they knead, sculpt, and bake the clay. In addition to using mud to make pottery, some Pueblo Indians apply mud to their bodies before they perform rituals.

People of the Middle East have used mineral-rich mud from the Dead Sea on their bodies since ancient times. The water that flows into this sea carries salt and minerals from surrounding regions. People believe that Dead Sea mud provides health and beauty benefits. Skin-care products made with Dead Sea mud are available in many parts of the world. Mud from other areas also is used for beauty treatments. In European spas, mud baths are a common form of treatment to relieve joint pain, relax muscles, increase circulation, and improve the condition of the skin. Algae, kelp, herbs, and minerals are other ingredients in these clay-based mud baths.

Reading Time ______

Recalling Facts

1. People use adobe bricks as a
   - ❑ a. way to prevent erosion.
   - ❑ b. beauty aid.
   - ❑ c. building material.

2. Mud is found
   - ❑ a. anywhere there is soil and water.
   - ❑ b. only where there are deposits of clay.
   - ❑ c. mainly along rivers.

3. Pottery is made from
   - ❑ a. mineral-rich mud.
   - ❑ b. sun-baked straw.
   - ❑ c. fired clay.

4. According to the article, the ancient Romans used baked clay for the construction of
   - ❑ a. water pipes.
   - ❑ b. statues.
   - ❑ c. roadways.

5. One reason that beauty spas provide mud baths is to
   - ❑ a. condition the skin.
   - ❑ b. relieve insect bites.
   - ❑ c. make people sweat to help them lose weight.

Understanding Ideas

6. From the article, one can infer that mud
   - ❑ a. is common in few places.
   - ❑ b. is limited to a few uses.
   - ❑ c. has changed little over time.

7. It is likely that ancient Egyptians used straw to make adobe bricks because the straw made the bricks more
   - ❑ a. fragile.
   - ❑ b. sturdy.
   - ❑ c. soft.

8. One can infer that businesses that make adobe bricks bake them in ovens because
   - ❑ a. it makes the bricks stronger.
   - ❑ b. there is not enough room to dry the bricks in the sun.
   - ❑ c. it is illegal to dry the bricks in the sun.

9. One can conclude from the article that mud was useful to many cultures throughout history because it was
   - ❑ a. a plentiful natural material.
   - ❑ b. the only material available.
   - ❑ c. not harmful to the environment.

10. One can conclude from the article that people use mud today to
    - ❑ a. create Egyptian architecture.
    - ❑ b. learn about ancient times.
    - ❑ c. meet health, beauty, and building needs.

11 B Preparing Adobe Bricks

Adobe bricks are sun-dried mud bricks. They can be prepared in two weeks in arid climates, but they take longer to prepare in moist climates. You can make adobe bricks with the following materials: dirt, water, a trash can, sand, straw, wood, a hammer, nails, oil, a shovel, and a hoe.

To prepare the bricks, use the shovel or the hoe to blend a thick paste of water and dirt in a trash can or barrel. If the dirt has a high clay content, add small quantities of sand and straw to the mixture in order to reduce the shrinkage and cracking of bricks. It is important to blend the mixture thoroughly and allow it to stand overnight to eliminate lumps.

In the meantime, using a hammer and nails, construct wooden forms in the shape of a shoebox without a bottom or top. Coat the completed wooden forms with inexpensive oil to prevent the drying adobe from sticking to them.

Once the mud mixture has set, place the wooden forms on dry, level ground and sprinkle sand in the bottom of each form. Scoop the adobe mixture into the forms, allow it to set for several hours, and then remove the forms. After three days, turn the bricks on their edges and let them dry for an additional three days. Store the bricks for another week of drying. The bricks can then be used to build walls, adobe ovens, or other structures.

1. Recognizing Words in Context

Find the word *arid* in the passage. One definition below is closest to the meaning of that word. One definition has the opposite or nearly opposite meaning. The remaining definition has a completely different meaning. Label the definitions C for *closest,* O for *opposite or nearly opposite,* and D for *different.*

_____ a. wet

_____ b. dry

_____ c. cold

2. Distinguishing Fact from Opinion

Two of the statements below present *facts,* which can be proved correct. The other statement is an *opinion,* which expresses someone's thoughts or beliefs. Label the statements F for *fact* and O for *opinion.*

_____ a. Adding sand and straw can help reduce cracking in adobe bricks.

_____ b. Coating wooden forms with oil helps prevent sticking.

_____ c. Making adobe bricks is difficult.

3. Keeping Events in Order

Label the statements below 1, 2, and 3 to show the order in which the steps should be performed.

______ a. Scoop the mud mixture into the forms.

______ b. Sprinkle sand into the wooden forms.

______ c. Mix dirt and water to form a thick paste.

4. Making Correct Inferences

Two of the statements below are correct *inferences,* or reasonable guesses. They are based on information in the passage. The other statement is an incorrect, or faulty, inference. Label the statements C for *correct* inference and F for *faulty* inference.

______ a. It takes years of training to make adobe bricks well.

______ b. Properly made adobe bricks are strong enough to use in many building projects.

______ c. Making adobe bricks involves several steps completed over a period of time.

5. Understanding Main Ideas

One of the statements below expresses the main idea of the passage. One statement is too general, or too broad. The other explains only part of the passage; it is too narrow. Label the statements M for *main idea,* B for *too broad,* and N for *too narrow.*

______ a. People can choose from a variety of natural materials to use in construction.

______ b. Adobe bricks can be made from basic materials by following a set of steps.

______ c. Sand and straw should be added if the mud contains a lot of clay.

Correct Answers, Part A ______

Correct Answers, Part B ______

Total Correct Answers ______

12 A The Origin of Seashells

Seashells—in their many sizes, shapes, and colors—are created by a fascinating assortment of marine creatures. A person walking along the seashore may find tiny, spiral-shaped shells; ridged shells shaped like fans; large, smooth shells covered in spots; and hinged shells that open and close. People have always admired shells as decorative objects, but to the animals that create them they are a matter of life and death.

Mollusks—which include clams, oysters, and sea snails—create some of the most familiar seashells. From the time they are larvae, mollusks produce calcium carbonate, a substance that hardens into layers on an area of skinlike material called a mantle. Over time, these layers build up and form a shell. The mollusk moves some of the calcium material to the edge of the shell so that the shell grows wider.

Mollusk shells serve to protect mollusks' soft bodies from predators and harsh conditions. For example, sea snails are well protected inside their hard one-piece shells. When it is safe, a snail can extend its foot through the opening of the shell to move and feed. If a predator is nearby or the snail is left in a dry area by the tide, a flap called the operculum closes over the shell's opening to protect the snail. Similarly, clams, mussels, and other mollusks called bivalves possess two-part hinged shells that can shut out danger. When safe from danger, bivalves can extend tubelike feet from their shells to feed and to burrow into the ocean's sandy bottom. If enemies approach or the bivalve is in danger of drying out on shore, muscles in its body hold the two halves of its shell tightly closed, keeping water in and enemies out.

Shells can protect their inhabitants from predators in other ways. The color, shape, and texture of shells can make it difficult for enemies to detect the shells or get hold of them. The patterns of some shells act as camouflage on the ocean bottom. Some creatures, such as the spiny oyster and the sea urchin, have sharp spines attached to their shells that discourage predators. Cowrie shells are so smooth and slippery that they are difficult for predators to grasp. If a predator does get hold of a sea creature's shell and manages to make a meal of the tender body inside, the empty shell remains behind as a reminder of its life.

Reading Time ______

Recalling Facts

1. Seashells are created by
   - ❑ a. ocean erosion.
   - ❑ b. pieces of fossils.
   - ❑ c. some kinds of marine animals.

2. To build its shell, a mollusk
   - ❑ a. glues sand together.
   - ❑ b. chews up rock.
   - ❑ c. produces calcium carbonate.

3. The patterns and colors of shells that can make a sea creature difficult to detect is an example of
   - ❑ a. symbolism.
   - ❑ b. camouflage.
   - ❑ c. metamorphosis.

4. Mollusks called ______ are able to tightly close their hinged shells when washed ashore.
   - ❑ a. bivalves
   - ❑ b. sea snails
   - ❑ c. squid

5. Mollusks build their shells over a skinlike area called the
   - ❑ a. flesh.
   - ❑ b. mantle.
   - ❑ c. foot.

Understanding Ideas

6. From the information in the article, one can infer that mollusks are most at danger when they are
   - ❑ a. very old.
   - ❑ b. in water near the shore.
   - ❑ c. larvae.

7. One can infer that the main reason that a bivalve opens its shell is to
   - ❑ a. get food.
   - ❑ b. dig into the sand.
   - ❑ c. breathe air.

8. The article suggests that a shell is most important in a marine animal's life for
   - ❑ a. attracting a mate.
   - ❑ b. absorbing food.
   - ❑ c. defense against enemies.

9. If a piece of a sea creature's shell is broken off, the creature will most likely
   - ❑ a. grow a new section of shell.
   - ❑ b. leave its shell and live in a rocky area.
   - ❑ c. find a new shell to inhabit.

10. Compared with a small-shelled clam, a large-shelled clam of the same species is most likely
    - ❑ a. healthier.
    - ❑ b. a male.
    - ❑ c. older.

12 B Common Shellfish

Shellfish form a regular part of the diet for people in many parts of the world. For many years, only people who lived near an ocean or other body of water ate shellfish. Today, however, modern transportation and refrigeration systems allow people in many other areas to enjoy shellfish. Some people do not eat shellfish because it is forbidden by their religion.

Two types of shellfish that humans eat are soft-bodied mollusks and hard-cased crustaceans. A variety of mollusks have become part of the human diet. Gastropods—such as the sea snail, abalone, and conch—are creatures with single shells that use a bellylike foot to move. The large bodies of some abalone and conch can be eaten as steaks. Clams, oysters, scallops, mussels, and other bivalves are more often eaten, because they are less expensive. Most mollusks live in salt water, but a few kinds live in fresh water. Some freshwater mollusks are endangered species. Although not usually considered a shellfish, the squid is a mollusk that is served in many restaurants. The squid has an internal platelike shell that bolsters its soft body from the inside out.

Lobsters, crabs, and shrimp are crustaceans that are popular in many countries. Unlike the shells of mollusks, their shells are like hard outer layers of skin coating their bodies. The shells are jointed to allow the animals to move rapidly in different directions.

1. Recognizing Words in Context

Find the word *bolsters* in the passage. One definition below is closest to the meaning of that word. One definition has the opposite or nearly opposite meaning. The remaining definition has a completely different meaning. Label the definitions C for *closest,* O for *opposite or nearly opposite,* and D for *different.*

______ a. supports

______ b. enlarges

______ c. weakens

2. Distinguishing Fact from Opinion

Two of the statements below present *facts,* which can be proved correct. The other statement is an *opinion,* which expresses someone's thoughts or beliefs. Label the statements F for *fact* and O for *opinion.*

______ a. People eat a variety of shellfish.

______ b. Fresh crab is delicious.

______ c. A lobster is a type of crustacean.

3. Keeping Events in Order

Label the statements below 1, 2, and 3 to show the order in which the events happen.

______ a. Many more people eat shellfish.

______ b. Only people who live near bodies of water eat shellfish.

______ c. The invention of refrigerated trucks and other vehicles allows shellfish to be widely distributed.

4. Making Correct Inferences

Two of the statements below are correct *inferences,* or reasonable guesses. They are based on information in the passage. The other statement is an incorrect, or faulty, inference. Label the statements C for *correct* inference and F for *faulty* inference.

______ a. Shellfish are similar types of creatures with little variety.

______ b. It is best to find out people's religious beliefs before serving them shellfish.

______ c. The term *shellfish* is mainly used when referring to animals that are used as food.

5. Understanding Main Ideas

One of the statements below expresses the main idea of the passage. One statement is too general, or too broad. The other explains only part of the passage; it is too narrow. Label the statements M for *main idea,* B for *too broad,* and N for *too narrow.*

______ a. Shellfish include gastropods and bivalves.

______ b. Today, people in many regions eat mollusks and crustaceans.

______ c. Animals that live in water are an important source of food for the human diet.

Correct Answers, Part A ______

Correct Answers, Part B ______

Total Correct Answers ______

13 A The Roles of Fruits and Seeds

Most plants reproduce by forming seeds. Flowering plants usually produce seeds that are contained in fruits. The scientific name for such a plant is *angiosperm.* The fruit covering makes seeds more likely to be scattered over a wide area by animals, wind, or water. A plant that grows in many areas is less likely to become extinct than one that grows in only one area. The fruit of an angiosperm is not necessarily something that people can eat. In this case, the word *fruit* simply refers to the mass of plant tissue that surrounds the seed. Some angiosperm fruits are actually poisonous.

Angiosperms depend on male and female flower parts to produce their seeds and fruits. At the center of the flower is the pistil, a female part that consists of a long column with a round base called an ovary. Inside the ovary are the tiny ovules that become seeds if they are fertilized. Fertilization occurs when pollen from a stamen, a male flower part, joins the ovule inside the ovary. Pollen that reaches the tip of the pistil grows a long tube down into the ovary. Once pollen joins the ovule inside the ovary, a seed begins to form, the ovary becomes a fruit, and the other flower parts wither and die.

The form of a fruit determines the manner in which seeds are scattered. For example, birds and other animals may eat soft, fleshy fruits, such as berries. These animals deposit the seeds in their waste, usually far from the parent plants. Some hard-shelled fruits that float—such as coconuts—are carried by water to faraway regions. Some other types of fruits rely on the wind to scatter their seeds. The milkweed bears fruit in the form of dry seedpods that grow until they burst. Once the seedpods burst, hundreds of seeds, each attached to many light, silken threads, are carried off by the wind.

No matter how much angiosperm fruits and seeds may differ, each seed contains the same blueprint for growth. Under the right conditions, the tiny embryo within the seed grows into a new plant. The embryo consists of a root, a shoot, and one or two seed-leaves called cotyledons, which provide food for the sprouting plant. As the seed sprouts, the root anchors the seedling in the earth, and the shoot grows up through the soil. As soon as the seedling penetrates the soil's surface, it begins to grow its first true leaves.

Reading Time ______

Recalling Facts

1. A type of flowering plant that produces seeds contained in a fruit is called
   - ❑ a. an angiosperm.
   - ❑ b. a gymnosperm.
   - ❑ c. a nonvascular plant.

2. Fertilization occurs in a flowering plant when
   - ❑ a. pollen joins with the ovule.
   - ❑ b. a bee gathers nectar.
   - ❑ c. a seed begins to sprout.

3. The part of a flower that provides pollen is the
   - ❑ a. petal.
   - ❑ b. fruit.
   - ❑ c. stamen.

4. The part of a flower that forms a fruit is called
   - ❑ a. pollen.
   - ❑ b. the ovary.
   - ❑ c. the stem.

5. A root, shoot, and cotyledon are contained in the part of a seed called
   - ❑ a. a stem.
   - ❑ b. an embryo.
   - ❑ c. a pistil.

Understanding Ideas

6. An example of a fruit formed by a flowering plant is
   - ❑ a. lettuce.
   - ❑ b. a petal on a rose.
   - ❑ c. a tomato.

7. The article suggests that the primary purpose of a fruit is to
   - ❑ a. help distribute seeds.
   - ❑ b. provide food for humans.
   - ❑ c. attract bees to a flower.

8. One can infer that pollen usually reaches the pistil either by being carried by an insect or by being
   - ❑ a. transported by rain.
   - ❑ b. distributed by a seed.
   - ❑ c. blown by the wind.

9. One can conclude that the seeds of wild plums would most likely be distributed by
   - ❑ a. animals.
   - ❑ b. wind.
   - ❑ c. water.

10. One can infer that seeds are least likely to be widely distributed if their fruits are
    - ❑ a. eaten by slow-moving animals.
    - ❑ b. heavy and poisonous.
    - ❑ c. on plants that grow in valleys.

13 B Using Plants to Make Natural Dyes

When Samantha had finished writing her science paper on natural dyes, she decided to make a bright cloth cover for the paper by using plant dyes. In her research, Samantha had found that people had used minerals, insects, and especially plants to make dyes since ancient times. Samantha set out to the store with her older sister Janel to buy some plants to use for dyes.

At the store, Samantha bought cranberries for red dye and a package of chopped red cabbage for blue dye. For yellow dye she bought turmeric, a spice made from a root. At home, Samantha and Janel heated the cranberries and the cabbage in water in separate iron pots for 30 minutes without allowing the water to boil. After turning off the stove, they let the pots stand overnight.

The next day, Janel helped Samantha strain the plant matter from the two pots and reheat the dyes. In a third pot, Samantha and Janel heated water and four tablespoons of turmeric powder. As the red, yellow, and blue dyes warmed up, Samantha, protected with oven mitts, used tongs to steep parts of a white handkerchief in the dyes. When she was done, she let the cloth cool and then rinsed it with cold water and hung it out to dry. Later, she fastened the rainbow-colored scarf to the cover of her paper.

1. Recognizing Words in Context

Find the word *steep* in the passage. One definition below is closest to the meaning of that word. One definition has the opposite or nearly opposite meaning. The remaining definition has a completely different meaning. Label the definitions C for *closest,* O for *opposite or nearly opposite,* and D for *different.*

_____ a. extend

_____ b. dry

_____ c. soak

2. Distinguishing Fact from Opinion

Two of the statements below present *facts,* which can be proved correct. The other statement is an *opinion,* which expresses someone's thoughts or beliefs. Label the statements F for *fact* and O for *opinion.*

_____ a. Red cabbage can be used to make a natural blue dye.

_____ b. People have made natural dyes since ancient times.

_____ c. Making natural dye is not worth the trouble.

3. **Keeping Events in Order**

Label the statements below 1, 2, and 3 to show the order in which the steps should be performed.

______ a. Rinse the cloth in cold water and hang it out to dry.

______ b. Soak the cloth in the heated dyes.

______ c. Prepare dyes by cooking plants in water for 30 minutes and allowing the pots to stand overnight.

4. **Making Correct Inferences**

Two of the statements below are correct *inferences,* or reasonable guesses. They are based on information in the passage. The other statement is an incorrect, or faulty, inference. Label the statements C for *correct* inference and F for *faulty* inference.

______ a. Many plant dyes are inexpensive to make.

______ b. All clothes colored with plant dye fade quickly.

______ c. One must be very careful when working with dyes because they can stain.

5. **Understanding Main Ideas**

One of the statements below expresses the main idea of the passage. One statement is too general, or too broad. The other explains only part of the passage; it is too narrow. Label the statements M for *main idea,* B for *too broad,* and N for *too narrow.*

______ a. Dyes are used to color clothing.

______ b. Cranberries can be used to make a red dye.

______ c. Plants can be used to make dyes for coloring cloth.

Correct Answers, Part A ______

Correct Answers, Part B ______

Total Correct Answers ______

14 A Computers Playing Chess and Solving Problems

Computers have the potential to answer some of the most important questions that scientists have about the universe. But in order for computers to reach this potential, scientists and engineers must design software and hardware that can work together as a system to solve challenging problems. The chess-playing supercomputer Deep Blue is one system that can serve as a model of just how much a computer can do.

Chess is a difficult game to play well because it requires different types of strategic and logical thinking. Yet is a game with rules that are easy for a computer to understand. A computer that can successfully combine the talents needed to play chess may have the capability to solve more important problems. Companies have been willing to invest large amounts of money and time to develop computers that play chess well.

The development of Deep Blue began in 1985, when two graduate students designed a computer system called Chiptest. Chiptest could examine a chess position by searching 50,000 chess moves per second and deciding which move was best. In the next few years, these same students made new models that could evaluate more than 500,000 chess moves per second and make better decisions. Expert chess players helped them, and they received funding from a major U.S. computer company. In 1989, their Deep Thought system won the World Computer Chess Championship with a perfect score. A few months later, however, Deep Thought was defeated with ease by Garry Kasparov, the top-ranked chess player in the world. After further improvements, the system, renamed Deep Blue, was able to assess more than 100 million chess moves per second. In 1997, Deep Blue defeated Kasparov in a six-game match. It became the first computer to defeat a human world champion under conditions similar to those of a chess tournament. Since then, a German software company has funded the development of a program called Deep Fritz that defeated other leading chess systems, including Deep Blue, at a computer tournament in 2001.

Deep Blue may have been designed to play chess, but in the process scientists learned how technology could be used to find solutions to complex problems. The technology used in the making of Deep Blue can be applied in a number of fields, including business and medicine. In late 2001, the U.S. company that funded Deep Blue announced Blue Gene/L, a project that would develop the most powerful supercomputer ever.

Reading Time ______

Recalling Facts

1. Chiptest was a computer system designed by two students in 1985 to
   - ❑ a. answer medical questions.
   - ❑ b. play chess.
   - ❑ c. develop business strategies.

2. Chiptest was replaced by a system called
   - ❑ a. Deep Thought.
   - ❑ b. Business Pro.
   - ❑ c. Chess Master.

3. Chess is a good problem for a computer to tackle because chess
   - ❑ a. uses rules that change during each part of the game.
   - ❑ b. requires fast play under strict time limits.
   - ❑ c. has fixed rules and requires strategic thinking.

4. Deep Blue became the first computer system to
   - ❑ a. win the computer chess championship seven years in a row.
   - ❑ b. defeat a human world champion.
   - ❑ c. play a chess game in less than five minutes.

5. A computer expected to be one of the fastest and most powerful supercomputers yet is
   - ❑ a. Blue Gene/L.
   - ❑ b. Chiptest.
   - ❑ c. Deep Thought.

Understanding Ideas

6. One can conclude from the article that Blue Gene/L will be
   - ❑ a. the last supercomputer.
   - ❑ b. followed by the development of even more powerful supercomputers.
   - ❑ c. the best chess player ever.

7. The article suggests that the technology used in the making of Deep Blue was developed to
   - ❑ a. promote the game of chess.
   - ❑ b. see how well computers could handle complex problems.
   - ❑ c. win millions of dollars in chess tournaments.

8. An unlikely use of supercomputers in the future is evaluating
   - ❑ a. child-care programs.
   - ❑ b. sales to increase business profits.
   - ❑ c. inherited characteristics linked to disease.

9. One can infer that one reason computer systems have improved at chess is that they can
   - ❑ a. study the mistakes made by other computers.
   - ❑ b. understand the way humans think.
   - ❑ c. analyze many moves in one second.

10. One can infer that the designers of the best computer chess systems need both supercomputers and
    - ❑ a. high-quality computer monitors.
    - ❑ b. complicated software programs.
    - ❑ c. advanced laptop computers.

14 B Are Computers Intelligent?

Chess is known as a game of intellect. If a computer can beat the world's best chess player, it seems logical to assume that the computer must be highly intelligent. This is not really the case. Although a computer does well at fixed problems such as chess, it lacks the range of intellect that humans have.

In a game of chess, for example, aspects of human intellect have allowed the best players to beat computers. Humans use strategy, pattern, and the ability to learn to overcome the computer's capacity for huge, high-speed searches. A human player can use the same pattern of moves to defeat some computers again and again. These machines fail to learn from their past mistakes unless humans change the software.

Although some of the more complex tasks of life—like chess—are easy for computers, some of the simplest tasks for humans are very hard for machines. This is because a computer lacks the range and level of intellect required to perform such tasks. Creating descriptive language and finding relationships between objects are tasks that even a young child masters. To a computer, however, these tasks pose difficulties. In effect, no computer is more intelligent than any human being regardless of whether the human is a newborn infant or a world-champion chess player.

1. Recognizing Words in Context

Find the word *capacity* in the passage. One definition below is closest to the meaning of that word. One definition has the opposite or nearly opposite meaning. The remaining definition has a completely different meaning. Label the definitions C for *closest,* O for *opposite or nearly opposite,* and D for *different.*

______ a. ability

______ b. utility

______ c. inability

2. Distinguishing Fact from Opinion

Two of the statements below present *facts,* which can be proved correct. The other statement is an *opinion,* which expresses someone's thoughts or beliefs. Label the statements F for *fact* and O for *opinion.*

______ a. Computers have trouble creating descriptive language.

______ b. A young child is better at learning language than a computer is.

______ c. Champion chess players are among the smartest people on Earth.

3. Keeping Events in Order

Label the statements below 1, 2, and 3 to show the order in which the events happen.

_____ a. A chess-playing computer fails to learn from a loss.

_____ b. A chess player defeats a computer by using an uncommon strategy.

_____ c. A chess-playing computer loses again because it does not learn from its mistakes.

4. Making Correct Inferences

Two of the statements below are correct *inferences,* or reasonable guesses. They are based on information in the passage. The other statement is an incorrect, or faulty, inference. Label the statements C for *correct* inference and F for *faulty* inference.

_____ a. Computers have no imagination.

_____ b. Humans can be more creative than computers can.

_____ c. Chess players are more intelligent than people who don't play chess are.

5. Understanding Main Ideas

One of the statements below expresses the main idea of the passage. One statement is too general, or too broad. The other explains only part of the passage; it is too narrow. Label the statements M for *main idea,* B for *too broad,* and N for *too narrow.*

_____ a. Computers have trouble learning from their mistakes.

_____ b. Computers lack the range of intelligence that humans have.

_____ c. Computers are very strong in some types of skills and weak in some other skills.

Correct Answers, Part A _____

Correct Answers, Part B _____

Total Correct Answers _____

15 A The Rocket: A Powerful Engine

Engines have many uses. One of the most common uses is to power transportation vehicles. For about 50 years, the rocket—the most powerful type of engine—has been used to power spacecraft. Rockets, however, have been used for many things besides spacecraft. The Chinese invented them more than a thousand years ago. They designed rockets for fireworks and later began using rockets as weapons. The development of rockets that could be used in spacecraft began in the early 1900s. Germany used rockets on large, long-distance missiles in World War II.

Rockets were first used successfully for space launches in the 1950s. In 1957, the Soviets launched the first satellite, *Sputnik 1,* into space. The following year, the United States launched its first satellite, *Explorer 1.* Each was launched by means of powerful rockets that had been designed as missiles.

Once rockets were able to reach space, a race was on to launch a human being into space. To achieve this feat, engineers needed to design more powerful rockets. This was because humans and their cargo required much heavier spacecraft. In 1961, the United States launched a Mercury craft into space with Alan Shepard aboard. The rocket used was not powerful enough, however, to allow Shepard to orbit the Earth as Yury Gagarin had done in the Soviet Vostok 1 spacecraft a month before. A year later, John Glenn became the first American to orbit Earth, in a Mercury spacecraft powered by an Atlas rocket.

After humans had flown in space, landing on the Moon became the next goal. To achieve this feat, astronauts would need an even heavier spacecraft and much more powerful rockets. In 1969, U.S. astronauts Neil Armstrong and Buzz Aldrin became the first humans to set foot on the Moon. They traveled in the spacecraft *Apollo 11,* powered by the most powerful rocket of the time, the *Saturn V.* Part of this spacecraft was a special moon-landing craft that required its own rockets.

Today U.S. space missions are carried out in spacecraft called space shuttles. Space shuttles are powered by three liquid-fuel rocket engines, as well as two solid rocket boosters used in takeoff. Each shuttle consists of these rockets, the airplane-shaped orbiter that houses the crew, and a huge external fuel tank that feeds the engines. The liquid-fuel rocket engines that power the space shuttles are the most advanced rockets ever built.

Reading Time ______

Recalling Facts

1. The first rockets were developed more than a thousand years ago in
   - ❑ a. Rome.
   - ❑ b. Egypt.
   - ❑ c. China.

2. The first satellites launched into space by the Soviet Union and the United States were
   - ❑ a. *Sputnik 1* and *Explorer 1.*
   - ❑ b. *Sputnik 1* and *Apollo 11.*
   - ❑ c. *Apollo 11* and *Saturn V.*

3. The first American to reach space could not orbit Earth because
   - ❑ a. the rocket was not powerful enough.
   - ❑ b. the rocket was too powerful.
   - ❑ c. there was no rocket.

4. A spacecraft that has three liquid-fueled rocket engines and two solid rocket boosters is
   - ❑ a. a satellite.
   - ❑ b. a space shuttle.
   - ❑ c. *Vostok 1.*

5. Neil Armstrong and Buzz Aldrin were the first astronauts to
   - ❑ a. land on Mars.
   - ❑ b. walk on the Moon.
   - ❑ c. orbit Earth.

Understanding Ideas

6. One can infer that the main reason that spacecraft require such powerful rockets is that
   - ❑ a. they must overcome the force of gravity.
   - ❑ b. spacecraft must travel at the speed of light.
   - ❑ c. rockets are needed for soft landings on Earth.

7. The article suggests that as rockets evolved from ancient to modern times they became
   - ❑ a. completely safe to use.
   - ❑ b. harder to control.
   - ❑ c. more powerful.

8. One can infer that rockets like those used for spacecraft could also be used for
   - ❑ a. fireworks.
   - ❑ b. long-distance missiles.
   - ❑ c. drag-racing cars.

9. Compared with the launch of a Mercury spacecraft, the launch of a shuttle requires
   - ❑ a. more powerful rockets.
   - ❑ b. thinner rockets.
   - ❑ c. the same rockets but with greater fuel supplies.

10. One can conclude from the article that advances in rocket technology are responsible for
    - ❑ a. most wars.
    - ❑ b. the success of the space program.
    - ❑ c. improved transportation.

15 B Ultraviolet Images of Space

There is more to space exploration than spacecraft and space travel. Scientists learn about Earth and the rest of the universe by studying stars, planets, and other objects in outer space. Special tools help make this possible. The far-ultraviolet camera is one such tool. This camera, invented by George Carruthers, has been used on spacecraft to take pictures of ultraviolet, or UV, light. This is the same harmful, invisible light that sunscreen helps to block.

A UV camera is a tool that has been efficacious in the study of space because hot objects in space give off UV light. By capturing this light, such a camera can create pictures of stars and clouds of dust and gas, giving scientists information that they cannot get on Earth. UV light from space is hard to detect on Earth because the atmosphere around the Earth blocks out most of these emissions. Carruthers's UV camera allows people to view the universe in new ways.

The camera has taken UV pictures from a number of points in space. Astronauts on the moon used it to take pictures of Earth, stars, and clouds of gas and dust. On another mission, the camera took UV pictures of a comet. In recent years, a research satellite equipped with the camera helped scientists to study Earth's outer atmosphere. From this site, the camera captured a UV image of a meteor passing through Earth's atmosphere.

1. Recognizing Words in Context

Find the word *efficacious* in the passage. One definition below is closest to the meaning of that word. One definition has the opposite or nearly opposite meaning. The remaining definition has a completely different meaning. Label the definitions C for *closest,* O for *opposite or nearly opposite,* and D for *different.*

______ a. useless

______ b. effective

______ c. focused

2. Distinguishing Fact from Opinion

Two of the statements below present *facts,* which can be proved correct. The other statement is an *opinion,* which expresses someone's thoughts or beliefs. Label the statements F for *fact* and O for *opinion.*

______ a. The far-ultraviolet camera is one of the most important inventions in the history of astronomy.

______ b. George Carruthers invented the far-ultraviolet camera.

______ c. UV images provide information about stars.

3. Keeping Events in Order

Label the statements below 1, 2, and 3 to show the order in which the events happen.

______ a. George Carruthers invents a UV camera.

______ b. Astronauts on the Moon use a UV camera.

______ c. Spacecraft carry a UV camera into space for the first time.

4. Making Correct Inferences

Two of the statements below are correct *inferences,* or reasonable guesses. They are based on information in the passage. The other statement is an incorrect, or faulty, inference. Label the statements C for *correct* inference and F for *faulty* inference.

______ a. Tools such as the UV camera have added a great deal to scientific knowledge of the universe.

______ b. Without a way to put UV cameras into space, scientists would find the cameras practically worthless.

______ c. UV cameras are used only in observatories on Earth to study the universe.

5. Understanding Main Ideas

One of the statements below expresses the main idea of the passage. One statement is too general, or too broad. The other explains only part of the passage; it is too narrow. Label the statements M for *main idea,* B for *too broad,* and N for *too narrow.*

______ a. George Carruthers's UV camera has provided valuable information about the universe.

______ b. Earth's atmosphere blocks most UV rays.

______ c. Astronauts have used special equipment in outer space to collect information about the universe.

Correct Answers, Part A ______

Correct Answers, Part B ______

Total Correct Answers ______

16 A George Washington Carver

Prior to the Civil War, the economy of the southern United States relied almost entirely on farming, especially the farming of cotton. Much of the cotton was grown by slaves on large plantations. After the war, economic conditions were difficult in the South. Former slaves rejoiced in their freedom but still faced discrimination and poor economic conditions. Many still worked on farms, and the destruction of resources during the war made farming difficult. During the 1890s, an insect called the boll weevil destroyed many cotton plants. In addition, growing only cotton had worn out the once-fertile soil. These struggles threatened not only the economy of the South but also industries of the North that depended on Southern farm products.

One person set out to solve these problems with science. George Washington Carver, born to slave parents near the end of the Civil War, was familiar with the problems of Southern farmers. Carver had grown up on a farm in Missouri and had gone on to study agricultural science. He spent his life as a teacher and researcher. He devised new uses for about 30 plants.

Carver did not confine his ideas to the classroom; he brought them directly to Southern farmers. He tried to help any farmers who were willing to listen. He taught farmers that decades of cotton growth had depleted their soil. He instructed them to plant another crop, such as peanuts, every second year to help replenish the soil. By rotating their crops—planting cotton one year and peanuts the next—farmers found that their soil improved. Then a new problem arose. At that time, peanuts were not thought to be very useful. Farmers could not find buyers for all the peanuts they grew.

Carver turned his research to finding new uses for peanuts and other plants that were good for the soil, such as sweet potatoes and pecans. Carver came up with 325 uses for peanuts, including the manufacture of many nonfood products. Cosmetics, dyes, paints, fuels, glues, inks, and medicines are just a few of the products that can be made from peanuts. Carver also found hundreds of uses for sweet potatoes and pecans, such as making pavement and substitutes for rubber. Despite his many inventions, Carver sought only three patents, for ways of making paints and stains from soybeans. Through his work, George Washington Carver helped to change the face of agriculture in the South.

Reading Time ______

Recalling Facts

1. Decades of cotton growth on Southern farmland
   - ❑ a. enriched soil.
   - ❑ b. wore out soil.
   - ❑ c. used up water sources.

2. Carver suggested that farmers plant peanuts, sweet potatoes, and pecans
   - ❑ a. alternately with cotton.
   - ❑ b. instead of cotton.
   - ❑ c. on new farms only.

3. Planting one crop one year and a different crop the next year is known as
   - ❑ a. crop rotation.
   - ❑ b. irrigation.
   - ❑ c. organic farming.

4. In the late 1800s, Southern economic resources were damaged by
   - ❑ a. decades of drought.
   - ❑ b. a 40-year recession.
   - ❑ c. the Civil War.

5. Carver found that peanuts could be used in such nonfood products as
   - ❑ a. stationery.
   - ❑ b. cosmetics and medicines.
   - ❑ c. wood-burning stoves.

Understanding Ideas

6. From the information in the article one can infer that
   - ❑ a. Southern farmers no longer grow cotton.
   - ❑ b. peanuts became an important crop in the South.
   - ❑ c. peanuts are now a more valuable crop than cotton is.

7. One can infer that without George Washington Carver Southern farmers today would be growing
   - ❑ a. fewer pecans and sweet potatoes.
   - ❑ b. no peanuts at all.
   - ❑ c. only cotton.

8. Compared with older farming methods, Carver's methods
   - ❑ a. decreased farm labor.
   - ❑ b. lowered the cost of food.
   - ❑ c. made soil more fertile.

9. One can conclude from the article that Carver had an important effect on the success of farming mainly because he
   - ❑ a. persuaded most Southern farmers to stop growing cotton.
   - ❑ b. invented useful products from crops that improved the soil.
   - ❑ c. sought patents for three of his inventions.

10. The article suggests that George Washington Carver
    - ❑ a. solved all of the important problems of Southern farmers.
    - ❑ b. worked hard for many years.
    - ❑ c. accomplished things that had little value.

16 B The Health Value of Nuts

Nuts provide a number of nutritional benefits. Like meat and beans, nuts are a great source of protein. Two tablespoons of peanut butter or one-third cup of nuts provides the same amount of protein as 29 grams (1 ounce) of lean meat.

Nuts also provide vitamins, minerals, and other substances that promote physical well-being. Pistachios are a good source of thiamin and vitamin B6. Almonds are an excellent source of vitamin E. Fiber, found in all nuts, helps to maintain the health of the digestive system. New research suggests that some chemicals in nuts may even help reduce the risk of cancer and heart disease.

Despite the high nutritional value of nuts, nutrition experts warn that nuts should be eaten only in small amounts because of their high fat content. A diet high in fat can lead to a number of health problems. In contrast to some other protein-rich foods, however, most of the fat in nuts is unsaturated fat. This form of fat is less harmful than saturated fat. In addition, unlike meat, nuts do not contain cholesterol, which promotes heart disease. In fact, some nuts, such as walnuts, can help control or even reduce cholesterol levels. Eaten in moderation, nuts are a healthful part of a balanced diet.

1. Recognizing Words in Context

Find the word *moderation* in the passage. One definition below is closest to the meaning of that word. One definition has the opposite or nearly opposite meaning. The remaining definition has a completely different meaning. Label the definitions C for *closest,* O for *opposite or nearly opposite,* and D for *different.*

______ a. a painful way

______ b. an excessive way

______ c. a limited way

2. Distinguishing Fact from Opinion

Two of the statements below present *facts,* which can be proved correct. The other statement is an *opinion,* which expresses someone's thoughts or beliefs. Label the statements F for *fact* and O for *opinion.*

______ a. Nuts are a protein-rich food source.

______ b. People who eat a handful of nuts several times a week are smart.

______ c. Nuts do not contain cholesterol.

3. Keeping Events in Order

Two of the statements below describe events that happened at the same time. The other statement describes an event that happened before or after those events. Label them S for *same time,* B for *before,* and A for *after.*

_____ a. A person's cholesterol level is a little too high.

_____ b. A person begins eating walnuts in moderation.

_____ c. A person's cholesterol level falls to an acceptable range.

4. Making Correct Inferences

Two of the statements below are correct *inferences,* or reasonable guesses. They are based on information in the passage. The other statement is an incorrect, or faulty, inference. Label the statements C for *correct* inference and F for *faulty* inference.

_____ a. Nuts have few nutritional benefits.

_____ b. Nuts contain more vitamins and minerals than meat does.

_____ c. One should not eat large amounts of nuts on a regular basis because of their high fat content.

5. Understanding Main Ideas

One of the statements below expresses the main idea of the passage. One statement is too general, or too broad. The other explains only part of the passage; it is too narrow. Label the statements M for *main idea,* B for *too broad,* and N for *too narrow.*

_____ a. High-protein foods include meat, beans, and nuts.

_____ b. Walnuts can reduce the risk of heart disease.

_____ c. When eaten in reasonable amounts, nuts are an important part of a healthful diet.

Correct Answers, Part A _____

Correct Answers, Part B _____

Total Correct Answers _____

17 A

A Monarch Butterfly's Life

The life cycle of the monarch butterfly has four stages. The monarch undergoes a complete change of form, or metamorphosis, from the time it begins life to the time it reaches maturity. Monarch butterflies are famous for their beauty and for the long-distance trips that some take in autumn.

In the first stage of the life cycle, the monarch is an egg. Female butterflies lay greenish eggs on the undersides of the leaves of just one type of plant—the milkweed. Milkweed also is the only plant that monarch caterpillars eat. Scientists refer to milkweed as a host plant for the monarch.

A caterpillar hatches from the egg and immediately begins to eat milkweed leaves. Within a few hours, the white caterpillar gains its characteristic black, yellow, and white stripes. During this second stage of the life cycle, the caterpillar eats almost all the time. It grows so much that it must molt, or shed its skin, four or five times. Before the final molting, the caterpillar starts to prepare for its next life stage.

The caterpillar spins silk to form a sort of net with a thick center, usually on the bottom of a twig or branch. The caterpillar then attaches itself to the center, called a silk button. From a hanging position, the caterpillar molts for the last time. Instead of forming a new skin, the creature becomes a pupa encased in a green and gold chrysalis.

In the third, or pupal, stage of life, the body of the caterpillar breaks down into a liquid inside the chrysalis. The liquid slowly reforms into a butterfly. In a week or two, the caterpillar with its 16 legs and 14 body segments has been transformed into a butterfly with 6 legs, 3 body sections, and a pair of orange and black wings.

After the butterfly emerges, it drinks nectar from flowers and looks for a mate. After mating, females lay their eggs. Most monarch butterflies accomplish this within a few weeks and then die. Butterflies that emerge at the end of summer, however, wait before mating. The milkweed leaves shrivel and die before the females are ready to lay their eggs. Monarchs born at this time migrate to Mexico or California for the winter because they cannot survive cold weather. In the spring they return to milkweed plants in the north to lay their eggs and start the life cycle anew.

Reading Time ______

Recalling Facts

1. The life cycle of a monarch butterfly has ______ stages.
   - ❑ a. five
   - ❑ b. three
   - ❑ c. four

2. The only plant upon which a female monarch butterfly lays eggs is the
   - ❑ a. buttercup.
   - ❑ b. tiger lily.
   - ❑ c. milkweed.

3. A monarch caterpillar eats only
   - ❑ a. silk.
   - ❑ b. leaves.
   - ❑ c. insects.

4. After a monarch caterpillar sheds its skin for the final time, it becomes
   - ❑ a. a pupa.
   - ❑ b. an egg.
   - ❑ c. a larva.

5. A monarch caterpillar is transformed into a butterfly inside
   - ❑ a. an egg.
   - ❑ b. a chrysalis.
   - ❑ c. a pod.

Understanding Ideas

6. From the information in the article, one can infer that monarch butterflies that migrate ______ those that don't migrate.
   - ❑ a. do not live as long as
   - ❑ b. live about as long as
   - ❑ c. live much longer than

7. One can conclude from the article that the size of the monarch butterfly population is limited mostly by
   - ❑ a. the number of milkweed plants.
   - ❑ b. long winter migrations.
   - ❑ c. an increased bird population.

8. It is likely that a monarch butterfly born in the springtime would lay eggs
   - ❑ a. after migrating south.
   - ❑ b. before fall.
   - ❑ c. in the winter.

9. One can infer that during their migration south monarch butterflies depend on ______ for food.
   - ❑ a. milkweed leaves
   - ❑ b. nectar
   - ❑ c. caterpillars

10. Compared with a butterfly, a monarch caterpillar
    - ❑ a. grows more.
    - ❑ b. feeds on pollen.
    - ❑ c. migrates farther.

17 B A Tour of the Butterfly Farm

Mr. Reyes welcomed the science class to the butterfly farm and explained the purpose of the farm. He said that butterflies were raised on the farm for the education of visitors, for release at special events, and for use in scientific research. After Mr. Reyes described some studies on migration that the farm staff was doing, he began the tour of the grounds.

First Mr. Reyes explained the four stages of a butterfly's life. Then he took the students to the farm's breeding grounds and showed them examples of each life stage. The class used magnifying glasses to examine monarch butterfly eggs on the undersides of milkweed leaves. Mr. Reyes pointed out caterpillars feeding on leaves and talked about their diet and body structure.

Next, Mr. Reyes explained the metamorphosis of the pupa within the chrysalis. On nearby plants, the students could discern pupae at different phases of change. They could also see the orange and black wings of a butterfly through one of the chrysalises. Mr. Reyes informed the class that this pupa would soon emerge to join the other butterflies around it.

Before the tour was over, Mr. Reyes showed the students a small garden of plants important to butterfly survival. He gave the class a gift of seeds and instructions so that they could plant their own butterfly garden and share what they had learned with others.

1. Recognizing Words in Context

Find the word *discern* in the passage. One definition below is closest to the meaning of that word. One definition has the opposite or nearly opposite meaning. The remaining definition has a completely different meaning. Label the definitions C for *closest,* O for *opposite or nearly opposite,* and D for *different.*

______ a. decide

______ b. notice

______ c. overlook

2. Distinguishing Fact from Opinion

Two of the statements below present *facts,* which can be proved correct. The other statement is an *opinion,* which expresses someone's thoughts or beliefs. Label the statements F for *fact* and O for *opinion.*

______ a. A visit to a butterfly farm is an excellent learning experience.

______ b. Butterflies pass through four stages of life.

______ c. Butterflies cannot survive without plants.

3. Keeping Events in Order

Label the statements below 1, 2, and 3 to show the order in which the events happen.

_____ a. The students examine a pupa.

_____ b. The students create their own butterfly garden to share what they've learned.

_____ c. The students use magnifying glasses to examine butterfly eggs.

4. Making Correct Inferences

Two of the statements below are correct *inferences,* or reasonable guesses. They are based on information in the passage. The other statement is an incorrect, or faulty, inference. Label the statements C for *correct* inference and F for *faulty* inference.

_____ a. A butterfly farm is a good place for rare species of butterflies to live.

_____ b. Workers at a butterfly farm must take good care of the plants there.

_____ c. Butterfly farms are always good places for monarchs to migrate in the fall.

5. Understanding Main Ideas

One of the statements below expresses the main idea of the passage. One statement is too general, or too broad. The other explains only part of the passage; it is too narrow. Label the statements M for *main idea,* B for *too broad,* and N for *too narrow.*

_____ a. A trip to a butterfly farm is an educational experience.

_____ b. Some scientists raise animals for purposes of research.

_____ c. A person can create a butterfly garden by growing certain types of plants.

Correct Answers, Part A _____

Correct Answers, Part B _____

Total Correct Answers _____

18 A The Importance of a Balanced Diet

For physical and mental health, it is important to eat a balanced diet. Studies have shown that a poor diet can contribute to many diseases and some mental disorders. A third of all cancers, for example, are related to poor diet, lack of fitness, or being overweight. Diet may also contribute to mood disorders such as depression and anxiety.

Eating provides the body with the energy and nutrients that allow it to function properly. Carbohydrates, fats, and proteins make up the three main chemical compounds found in food. All three are important for good health. Eating too much or too little from any category can have serious health consequences.

Carbohydrates consist of starches, sugars, and fiber. Starches and sugars are the main sources of energy for the body. Grains, vegetables, and fruits are rich in carbohydrates. These foods are broken down to glucose, which the body uses for energy. The energy from starches and sugars can be used right away or stored. If the body takes in too much starch or sugar, some is converted into fat. Fiber is important for a healthy digestive system. Nutritionists divide carbohydrates into two categories: simple and complex. A diet too rich in the simple carbohydrates, especially sugars, increases risks of disease and can cause mood swings.

Fats are foods that provide energy and lipids to the body. The lipids that make up fats are needed to create the membranes that form the borders of cells. Butter, oils, meats, and nuts are foods that are rich in fat. Fat that is not used is stored under the skin and between muscles and organs. A diet high in fat is not healthful, as it may lead to obesity and increase the risk of many diseases. Some types of fat, especially polyunsaturated fats and fatty acids, are beneficial to health.

Proteins are the building blocks of body tissue and enzymes. They are needed for proper growth and for body chemistry. Beans, eggs, nuts, meat, fish, and dairy products are good sources of protein.

Vitamins and minerals are also vital for physical and mental health. Calcium—found in dairy products, kale, and broccoli—keeps teeth and bones strong. Vitamin C, found in citrus fruits, keeps body tissues healthy and helps wounds heal. Some mood disorders may be a result of a lack of certain vitamins and minerals. A lack of riboflavin, vitamin B_{12}, calcium, zinc, or iron can cause depression.

Reading Time ______

Recalling Facts

1. Starches and sugars are
   - ❑ a. junk food.
   - ❑ b. carbohydrates.
   - ❑ c. fats.

2. Compounds that provide the body with lipids are
   - ❑ a. vitamins.
   - ❑ b. minerals.
   - ❑ c. fats.

3. Compounds that play a key role in the proper growth of the body are
   - ❑ a. proteins.
   - ❑ b. carbohydrates.
   - ❑ c. starches.

4. The three main compounds found in food are
   - ❑ a. starches, sugars, and fiber.
   - ❑ b. lipids, fiber, and enzymes.
   - ❑ c. proteins, fats, and carbohydrates.

5. Studies show that eating a balanced diet
   - ❑ a. decreases the risk of disease.
   - ❑ b. always results in weight loss.
   - ❑ c. permanently eliminates depression.

Understanding Ideas

6. One can conclude from the article that a well-balanced diet
   - ❑ a. contributes to mental and physical health.
   - ❑ b. cures diseases such as cancer.
   - ❑ c. increases fitness.

7. The article indicates that is best to eat
   - ❑ a. a large serving of one fatty food each day.
   - ❑ b. a small amount of fat each day.
   - ❑ c. no fat at all.

8. One can infer that eating large amounts of starchy food would result in
   - ❑ a. having twice as much energy.
   - ❑ b. an increase in body fat.
   - ❑ c. an increase in body growth.

9. It is likely that eating the same foods day after day would result in a
   - ❑ a. lack of some vitamins and minerals.
   - ❑ b. lack of fats.
   - ❑ c. well-balanced diet.

10. A balanced diet is most likely to be achieved with which of the following meals?
    - ❑ a. fish, a potato with margarine, and broccoli
    - ❑ b. scrambled eggs with ham and cheese
    - ❑ c. pasta salad and an apple

18 B The Need for Exercise

Studies show that regular exercise promotes good health. It helps to control weight, reduces depression, and keeps bones, muscles, and joints healthy. Exercise also lowers the risk of many diseases. Heart disease, cancer, and high blood pressure are less common in people who exercise regularly. Especially beneficial is aerobic exercise, which might include jogging or swimming for 30 minutes three or four times a week.

Even though people are aware of the value of exercise, more than 60 percent of the people in the United States are not active enough to maintain good health. Almost half of all American teens are not active enough. As teens get older, their average amount of exercise decreases.

To combat this problem, national programs promote youth exercise. Walk-to-school programs encourage students to get exercise in this simple manner. Many schools have improved their physical education programs. New parks and youth centers are planned throughout the United States. These programs offer youth ways to exercise on a regular basis.

Besides organized programs, there are many other ways for teens to stay active. Riding a bicycle for fun or to get from place to place each day is one way. Other ways include dancing to music with friends or climbing steps rather than taking an elevator. Exercise does not need to be strenuous to benefit health. Being physically active on a routine basis is what is important.

1. Recognizing Words in Context

Find the word *beneficial* in the passage. One definition below is closest to the meaning of that word. One definition has the opposite or nearly opposite meaning. The remaining definition has a completely different meaning. Label the definitions C for *closest,* O for *opposite or nearly opposite,* and D for *different.*

_____ a. helpful

_____ b. harmful

_____ c. tiring

2. Distinguishing Fact from Opinion

Two of the statements below present *facts,* which can be proved correct. The other statement is an *opinion,* which expresses someone's thoughts or beliefs. Label the statements F for *fact* and O for *opinion.*

_____ a. More than 60 percent of Americans do not get enough exercise.

_____ b. Exercise is fun and healthful.

_____ c. National programs promote youth exercise.

3. Keeping Events in Order

Two of the statements below describe events that happen at the same time. The other statement describes an event that happens before or after those events. Label them S for *same time,* B for *before,* or A for *after.*

_____ a. Risk of heart disease is lowered.

_____ b. Bones, muscles, and joints remain healthy.

_____ c. An inactive person begins a program of light exercise.

4. Making Correct Inferences

Two of the statements below are correct *inferences,* or reasonable guesses. They are based on information in the passage. The other statement is an incorrect, or faulty, inference. Label the statements C for *correct* inference and F for *faulty* inference.

_____ a. Many teenagers in the United States are not as healthy as they should be.

_____ b. To aid health, exercise must be done regularly.

_____ c. Playing video games is a good form of exercise.

5. Understanding Main Ideas

One of the statements below expresses the main idea of the passage. One statement is too general, or too broad. The other explains only part of the passage; it is too narrow. Label the statements M for *main idea,* B for *too broad,* and N for *too narrow.*

_____ a. Fitness is a key to good health, but many people do not get enough exercise.

_____ b. Swimming is a form of aerobic exercise.

_____ c. It is possible for people to become healthier.

Correct Answers, Part A _____

Correct Answers, Part B _____

Total Correct Answers _____

19 A

The Importance of Trees

Trees are precious natural resources that benefit people in a number of ways. People depend on trees for wood, paper, food, medicine, and many other products. Most importantly, trees help to create the environmental conditions that support life on Earth.

Throughout the world, people use wood and paper products. Lumber is used to construct buildings, to make cabinets and furniture, and to build fences and decks. Most of the lumber that people use to build houses in the United States comes from tall evergreen trees in the western part of the country. Hardwood trees from several regions provide wood for furniture. Ground-up wood called pulp is used to make paper. Cork, made from the bark of the cork oak tree, is used in many products.

Not only does wood provide many useful products, but it also serves as a fuel for heating and cooking. Almost half of the world's population depends on wood as a main source of energy. In addition to home use, many industries rely on wood fuel—especially charcoal, which is made from wood.

Trees are a valuable food source as well. Some tree parts, especially fruits and nuts, are edible. Farmers grow orchards of fruit trees and nut trees. For some people, forest plants and animals are key food sources that would not survive without trees.

Trees also provide valuable medicines. The native peoples of the Amazon rain forest use more than a thousand different forest plants for medicine. Not all of the medicines come from trees, but without the unique environment provided by the trees of the rain forest, other rain forest plants would not be able to grow. Some trees do provide medicine. Although most of the aspirin produced today is made in laboratories, it originally was obtained from the bark of the white willow tree.

Trees are most important, however, for helping to create favorable environmental conditions for other living things. Trees absorb carbon dioxide, which in high concentrations is harmful to animals. Trees also give off oxygen, which is essential for life. Tree roots help soil absorb more water, and they also help to prevent soil from washing away. This benefits other plants. Similarly, trees and their roots help to prevent flooding by keeping water from washing too quickly into streams and rivers. By maintaining the conditions of Earth's environment in these ways, trees sustain the lives of organisms around the world.

Reading Time ______

Recalling Facts

1. A product that comes from trees is
   - ❑ a. brick.
   - ❑ b. cork.
   - ❑ c. glass.

2. Most of the lumber used to build houses in the United States comes from the _____ part of the country.
   - ❑ a. western
   - ❑ b. eastern
   - ❑ c. southern

3. A wood product that many industries rely on for fuel is
   - ❑ a. pulp.
   - ❑ b. charcoal.
   - ❑ c. pine needles.

4. More than _____ different plants of the Amazon rain forest provide medicines for native peoples.
   - ❑ a. 1,000,000
   - ❑ b. 100,000
   - ❑ c. 1,000

5. Trees sustain the lives of all creatures on Earth mainly by
   - ❑ a. helping to maintain environmental conditions.
   - ❑ b. serving as the main source of food.
   - ❑ c. providing wood and paper.

Understanding Ideas

6. It is likely that a sudden huge decrease in the number of trees on Earth would
   - ❑ a. increase oxygen levels.
   - ❑ b. decrease oxygen levels.
   - ❑ c. create severe drought.

7. One can infer from the information in the article that most of the trees that are cut down are used for
   - ❑ a. lumber.
   - ❑ b. fuel.
   - ❑ c. food.

8. One could conclude from the article that the kinds of product obtained from trees
   - ❑ a. is determined solely by a tree's location.
   - ❑ b. is consistent across all trees.
   - ❑ c. varies according to the type of tree.

9. The use of which tree product would be least likely to harm trees?
   - ❑ a. food
   - ❑ b. pulp
   - ❑ c. furniture

10. One reason a city government might want to plant trees would be to
   - ❑ a. produce carbon dioxide.
   - ❑ b. improve air quality.
   - ❑ c. provide new medicines.

19 B The Problem of Deforestation

The term *deforestation* refers to the destruction of forests. The loss of forests affects climate, soil, water flow, and the diversity of life forms on Earth. Most deforestation occurs because of human activities. Countries have found it difficult to balance people's economic needs with the need to conserve forests for their environmental benefits. As the world's population has increased, people have cut down forests to build roads, construct houses, and plant crops. People also cut down trees for the valuable products they provide.

One proposal for limiting deforestation is to have people harvest forest products that do not require trees to be cut down. In the rain forests of Brazil, some trees provide sap from which rubber can be made. Forests also can provide such valuable products as coffee and fruit.

These solutions, however, cannot by themselves solve the problem of deforestation. People depend on logging to provide wood products. Logging is very difficult to stop, but it can be managed in a way that causes less harm to a forest. Scientists study the whole landscape of a forest to learn how the loss of trees will affect the region. Then they identify sections of forest where logging can be allowed. Young trees are planted in areas where logging has occurred. With proper management, forests will be able to meet human needs while continuing to benefit all of Earth's living things.

1. Recognizing Words in Context

Find the word *diversity* in the passage. One definition below is closest to the meaning of that word. One definition has the opposite or nearly opposite meaning. The remaining definition has a completely different meaning. Label the definitions C for *closest,* O for *opposite or nearly opposite,* and D for *different.*

______ a. harmony

______ b. variety

______ c. sameness

2. Distinguishing Fact from Opinion

Two of the statements below present *facts,* which can be proved correct. The other statement is an *opinion,* which expresses someone's thoughts or beliefs. Label the statements F for *fact* and O for *opinion.*

______ a. Rubber is made from the sap of some trees.

______ b. People clear forests so that they can build houses and plant crops.

______ c. Deforestation is the biggest environmental problem in the world today.

3. Keeping Events in Order

Label the statements below 1, 2, and 3 to show the order in which the events happen.

______ a. People cut down trees without destroying a forest.

______ b. Scientists carefully study an entire forest.

______ c. Scientists recommend a section of the forest where logging will do the least damage.

4. Making Correct Inferences

Two of the statements below are correct *inferences,* or reasonable guesses. They are based on information in the passage. The other statement is an incorrect, or faulty, inference. Label the statements C for *correct* inference and F for *faulty* inference.

______ a. If people make a determined effort, deforestation can be completely eliminated.

______ b. Deforestation can be controlled through forest management.

______ c. The continued loss of forests will result in the extinction of plants and animals.

5. Understanding Main Ideas

One of the statements below expresses the main idea of the passage. One statement is too general, or too broad. The other explains only part of the passage; it is too narrow. Label the statements M for *main idea,* B for *too broad,* and N for *too narrow.*

______ a. Environmental problems are often the result of human activities.

______ b. Forests provide valuable products other than wood.

______ c. People can control deforestation in several ways.

Correct Answers, Part A ______

Correct Answers, Part B ______

Total Correct Answers ______

20 A Large Dams: Benefits or Burdens?

For thousands of years, people have tried to control water by building dams. Dams allow people to collect and store water for use at home, in industry, and in agriculture. For example, when people build a dam on a river, a reservoir collects water that can be channeled for human needs. In addition, the ability of dams to control water flow helps prevent floods. Dams can also be used to generate electricity.

As the human population grows, the need for water and electricity increases. For this reason, many new dams have been built in the past 50 years. Today, nearly half of the rivers in the world have at least one large dam. If managed well, dams can be a great benefit to people. Some dams, however, may do more harm than good.

All dams cause changes in a river ecosystem that have an impact on surrounding land and people. As river water collects in a reservoir behind a large dam, it may back up and form a large lake, flooding land and killing plants and animals. People living on land upstream of a dam may be forced to abandon their homes. Below the dam, water flow decreases. This changes the downstream ecosystem. Plants and animals may not have enough water. Some types of fish may be unable to move upstream to reproduce. Rare species of plants and animals may become endangered. Farmers living downstream from the dam may not be able to grow crops. People who fish for a living may have to find other work. Opposition to large dams has grown as a result of these problems.

An independent organization called the World Commission on Dams worked during the late 1990s to suggest ways of reducing problems caused by some large dams. The commission recommended that research, group decision making, and the creation of a plan all take place before the start of construction on a large dam. For a plan to be successful, it would need to demonstrate that the dam would contribute to the long-term improvement of human life. The likely impact of the dam on local people and the environment would be assessed and considered in the decision-making process. If the dam would create too much hardship for people, or if it would do too much damage to the environment, the planners would look for alternatives that could provide the benefis of a dam while placing less of a burden on the region.

Reading Time ______

Recalling Facts

1. Dams allow for the collection of water and the control of
   - ❑ a. water flow.
   - ❑ b. wildlife.
   - ❑ c. electricity.

2. Large dams can help prevent
   - ❑ a. floods.
   - ❑ b. extinction of wildlife.
   - ❑ c. drought.

3. Problems caused by dams are a result of
   - ❑ a. heavy rains.
   - ❑ b. changes to surrounding ecosystems.
   - ❑ c. electricity shortages.

4. People living downstream from a dam
   - ❑ a. receive the most benefits.
   - ❑ b. are able to obtain more water for farming and agriculture.
   - ❑ c. may not be able to fish or grow crops.

5. The World Commission on Dams recommended that before construction starts on a large dam
   - ❑ a. all endangered species be moved.
   - ❑ b. a plan be created.
   - ❑ c. people affected by the dam be given money.

Understanding Ideas

6. The article suggests that opposition to large dams has developed because
   - ❑ a. the negative effects of dams have sometimes been ignored.
   - ❑ b. dams have not been effective in reducing flooding.
   - ❑ c. of the high costs of maintaining larger dams.

7. The article suggests that large numbers of dams have been built in the past 50 years mainly because of
   - ❑ a. increased flood problems.
   - ❑ b. a growth in population, industry, and agriculture.
   - ❑ c. critical shortages of electricity.

8. Unlike poorly planned dams, carefully planned dams offer
   - ❑ a. no environmental harm.
   - ❑ b. electricity for entire countries.
   - ❑ c. great benefits and fewer burdens for people and the environment.

9. One can infer that to meet the guidelines of the World Commission on Dams a plan for a large dam would need to
   - ❑ a. consider the effects of the dam many years into the future.
   - ❑ b. focus on damage done by the construction of the dam.
   - ❑ c. make fish the main concern.

10. One can infer that in the future
    - ❑ a. the most harmful dams will be eliminated.
    - ❑ b. many more dams will be built.
    - ❑ c. only dams that do no damage to the environment will be constructed.

20 B Sharing Water from the Hoover Dam

One of the world's largest dams is the Hoover Dam, in the southwestern United States. The dam, completed in 1935, collects water from the Colorado River for the people of seven states. In 1921, during the planning of the dam, U.S. Secretary of Commerce Herbert Hoover was asked to resolve disputes between the states about how much river water each could use. This water supply was invaluable because of the region's dry climate.

When at first the states were unable to agree on how to allocate the water, Hoover proposed a compromise. He suggested that the region around the dam be divided into upper and lower basins. The upper basin would provide water to New Mexico, Wyoming, Colorado, and Utah. The lower basin would serve Nevada, Arizona, and California. The states also agreed to work out the details at a later time. The Colorado River Compact was signed in 1922, and plans for the dam proceeded. Eventually, the dam was named after Hoover, who became president of the United States during its construction.

Despite the signed agreement, states were not able to resolve their water disputes even after the dam was built. Finally, in 1948 the upper basin states settled their dispute. The lower basin states, however, were not able to reach an agreement. In the end, the U.S. Supreme Court decided the case some 40 years after the signing of the original compact.

1. Recognizing Words in Context

Find the word *allocate* in the passage. One definition below is closest to the meaning of that word. One definition has the opposite or nearly opposite meaning. The remaining definition has a completely different meaning. Label the definitions C for *closest,* O for *opposite or nearly opposite,* and D for *different.*

_____ a. combine

_____ b. divide up

_____ c. find

2. Distinguishing Fact from Opinion

Two of the statements below present *facts,* which can be proved correct. The other statement is an *opinion,* which expresses someone's thoughts or beliefs. Label the statements F for *fact* and O for *opinion.*

_____ a. The Hoover Dam was completed in 1935.

_____ b. The states involved in the dispute did not behave reasonably.

_____ c. Seven states were involved in the dispute.

3. Keeping Events in Order

Label the statements below 1, 2, and 3 to show the order in which the events happened.

_____ a. Herbert Hoover proposed a compromise when states could not agree on how Colorado River water should be shared.

_____ b. The Supreme Court decided the case for the lower-basin states.

_____ c. The Colorado River Compact was signed in 1922.

4. Making Correct Inferences

Two of the statements below are correct *inferences,* or reasonable guesses. They are based on information in the passage. The other statement is an incorrect, or faulty, inference. Label the statements C for *correct* inference and F for *faulty* inference.

_____ a. Some of the people who were most concerned about the water dispute were farmers.

_____ b. An agreement proposed by Herbert Hoover allowed the building of the dam to proceed, but that did not completely resolve the states' dispute.

_____ c. Without the Colorado River Compact, the states never would have agreed on how to share the water.

5. Understanding Main Ideas

One of the statements below expresses the main idea of the passage. One statement is too general, or too broad. The other explains only part of the passage; it is too narrow. Label the statements M for *main idea,* B for *too broad,* and N for *too narrow.*

_____ a. Dividing the water from the Hoover Dam among different states was an issue that took decades to resolve.

_____ b. A proposal by Herbert Hoover led to the Colorado River Compact.

_____ c. Water is a valuable natural resource.

Correct Answers, Part A _____

Correct Answers, Part B _____

Total Correct Answers _____

21 A How Magnets Work

A magnet is a piece of metal or rock that attracts and repels objects that contain magnetic material. Some magnets are manufactured. Lodestone, a type of rock made up of iron ore, is one kind of natural magnet.

The movements of charged particles called electrons create magnetic force. Electrons are part of atoms. The movement of electrons within an atom causes one part of an atom to have a positive charge and another part to have a negative charge. Therefore, an atom can be described as having a north (positive) pole and a south (negative) pole.

A magnet's atoms are lined up so that all the north poles point in the same direction and all the south poles point in the other direction. The two ends of the magnet that the poles are pointing toward have the strongest magnetic force. One end has a positive charge, and the other end has a negative charge. The negative end of one magnet will attract, or pull on, the positive end of another magnet. Two positive ends will repel, or push against, each other. So will two negative ends. The closer that two magnets are to each other, the stronger these forces are.

In objects that are not magnetic, the poles of the atoms face in many different directions, and the forces cancel one another out. If an object contains some magnetic material, however, the force of a magnet will cause the poles of the object's atoms to line up. The object will become a temporary magnet. For example, paper clips can be suspended in a chain from a magnet because each paper clip acts as a temporary magnet.

People use magnets in many ways. Because Earth itself is a weak magnet, magnets are useful for navigation. The needle of a compass is a magnet that points north by lining up with Earth's magnetic field. Other types of magnets are used in electrical devices or to produce electricity. When a wire is wound around an iron rod and an electric current is sent through the wire, the rod becomes a temporary magnet. This type of magnet, called an electromagnet, is used in devices such as doorbells and telephones. Just as electricity can be used to create magnets, magnets can be used to create electricity. A turbine is a machine in which flowing steam or water causes a large coil of wire to turn between two magnets and create electricity.

Reading Time ______

Recalling Facts

1. The parts of magnets with the strongest pushing and pulling forces are
   - ❑ a. the centers.
   - ❑ b. the red parts.
   - ❑ c. the ends.

2. Magnetic charges are caused mainly by forces in
   - ❑ a. atoms.
   - ❑ b. air.
   - ❑ c. soil.

3. The positive end of one magnet will ______ the positive end of another magnet.
   - ❑ a. attract
   - ❑ b. repel
   - ❑ c. have no effect on

4. Because Earth is a weak magnet, magnets are especially valuable in
   - ❑ a. navigation.
   - ❑ b. farming.
   - ❑ c. mining.

5. Some doorbells contain
   - ❑ a. turbines.
   - ❑ b. electromagnets.
   - ❑ c. compasses.

Understanding Ideas

6. A plastic bottle would not be attracted to a magnet because
   - ❑ a. the bottle does not have an electric current.
   - ❑ b. the bottle does not contain magnetic material.
   - ❑ c. the poles of the bottle's atoms do not face in different directions.

7. One can infer that in a permanent magnet
   - ❑ a. the poles of the atoms are permanently lined up in the same direction.
   - ❑ b. the material was at one time exposed to a massive electric current.
   - ❑ c. the positive end repels the negative end.

8. From the information in the article, one can infer that a material that contains ______ is likely to have magnetic properties.
   - ❑ a. red paint
   - ❑ b. iron
   - ❑ c. nitrogen

9. If a paper clip becomes a temporary magnet, one end of the paper clip will have a negative charge, and the other end will have
   - ❑ a. a positive charge.
   - ❑ b. no charge.
   - ❑ c. a negative charge.

10. From the article, one can infer that ______ have strong magnetic forces.
    - ❑ a. wooden boats
    - ❑ b. electric power lines
    - ❑ c. cement sidewalks

21 B A Compass Treasure Hunt

To prepare for the Outdoor Club's next wilderness trip, Sandra, the club president, had organized a treasure hunt in a forest at a local park. The treasure hunt would give the club members practice in using a compass. Each team received a different set of directions leading to the hidden treasure. To follow one set of directions, members would need to use the four cardinal points of the compass—north, east, south, and west—as well as the secondary points, such as northeast and southwest. For the second set of directions, members would need to use the degree markings on the compass.

At the starting point, Jack and his team began to read their instructions: "First, take 25 paces northeast." Maria held the compass and waited for the needle to settle on the north-south line. Team members found their bearing and headed 25 paces into the woods.

Meanwhile, the other team set out on the course, using the second set of directions. Sandra heard the team members calculating their first move: "First, take 30 paces at 120 degrees." They disappeared into the woods, counting out their paces aloud. Later, Sandra heard Jack, Maria, and their teammates shouting in victory as they emerged with the hidden treasure—a box of energy bars for the next week's wilderness trip.

1. Recognizing Words in Context

Find the word *cardinal* in the passage. One definition below is closest to the meaning of that word. One definition has the opposite or nearly opposite meaning. The remaining definition has a completely different meaning. Label the definitions C for *closest,* O for *opposite or nearly opposite,* and D for *different.*

_____ a. minor

_____ b. main

_____ c. red

2. Distinguishing Fact from Opinion

Two of the statements below present *facts,* which can be proved correct. The other statement is an *opinion,* which expresses someone's thoughts or beliefs. Label the statements F for *fact* and O for *opinion.*

_____ a. A compass is marked with cardinal and secondary points.

_____ b. The cardinal points on a compass are north, east, south, and west.

_____ c. It is difficult to use a compass to navigate by degrees.

3. Keeping Events in Order

Label the statements below 1, 2, and 3 to show the order in which the events happen.

_____ a. The teams use compass directions to help them look for a treasure.

_____ b. Jack's team finds a box of energy bars.

_____ c. Sandra plans a treasure hunt for the Outdoor Club.

4. Making Correct Inferences

Two of the statements below are correct *inferences,* or reasonable guesses. They are based on information in the passage. The other statement is an incorrect, or faulty, inference. Label the statements C for *correct* inference and F for *faulty* inference.

_____ a. Most people need practice to use a compass well.

_____ b. Jack and his teammates found the treasure first because their directions were easier.

_____ c. A compass is a useful tool when navigating in the wilderness.

5. Understanding Main Ideas

One of the statements below expresses the main idea of the passage. One statement is too general, or too broad. The other explains only part of the passage; it is too narrow. Label the statements M for *main idea,* B for *too broad,* and N for *too narrow.*

_____ a. Several devices can be used for navigation.

_____ b. Compasses show the cardinal points.

_____ c. A treasure hunt gives club members practice in using a compass.

Correct Answers, Part A _____

Correct Answers, Part B _____

Total Correct Answers _____

22 A Plant Adaptations

Plants grow in almost every region of the world. They can grow in climates that are hot or cold and in climates that are humid or dry. Over millions of years, plants have been able to adapt to extreme conditions and sometimes even thrive in them.

In regions with four seasons, most plants grow only during those seasons that provide sufficient sunlight, warmth, and water. During cold winters, plants are likely to be dormant, or inactive. To prepare for the cold, some trees and bushes shed their leaves, which are easily damaged by freezing temperatures. Because bacteria and fungi can attack damaged leaves and harm the other main parts of the plant, leaves are shed before cold weather arrives. A protective seal called a leaf scar forms at the point where the leaf was connected to the plant.

In the Arctic tundra, where the ground is completely frozen for most of the year, some plants manage to survive. Their roots grow just below the soil's surface, where thawing occurs the earliest. Strong, bitter winds are common on the tundra, so only plants that grow close to the ground in compact clumps can resist freezing there. Their roots may not grow deep, but they extend over a wide area to keep the plants firmly anchored. These plants, like plants in other icy climates, grow and store food during the fleeting warm season and are dormant in the cold months.

In contrast, most desert plants are dormant during the hottest time of the year. Because the desert is so dry and hot, water loss is the biggest threat to plants' survival. Cacti have developed thick, waxy skins that help to prevent water from evaporating into the air. Other desert plants, such as annual wildflowers, survive heat and drought in the form of seeds. When sufficient rain falls at a cooler time of year, these seeds grow into plants that can produce seeds of their own in just a few weeks. Seeds can lie dormant in desert soil for years until conditions are right for growth.

For plants that grow in tropical rain forests, there is no need to become dormant. Conditions there are always right for plant growth, as long as the soil drains well. Plants must compete with other plants for space and access to sunlight. Small plants called epiphytes secure access to sunlight by growing on larger plants, especially trees, and collecting water from the air.

Reading Time ______

Recalling Facts

1. During cold winters, most plants
   - ❑ a. grow and store food.
   - ❑ b. are dormant.
   - ❑ c. produce new leaves.

2. Plants survive the severe winds in the Arctic tundra by growing
   - ❑ a. close to the ground.
   - ❑ b. tall and sturdy as trees do.
   - ❑ c. very deep roots.

3. A common threat to desert plants is
   - ❑ a. dormancy.
   - ❑ b. bright sunlight.
   - ❑ c. water loss.

4. Wildflowers in the desert survive heat and drought
   - ❑ a. by producing seeds.
   - ❑ b. by growing thorns.
   - ❑ c. by shedding their leaves.

5. An epiphyte is a rain-forest plant that grows
   - ❑ a. on the forest floor.
   - ❑ b. underground.
   - ❑ c. on other plants.

Understanding Ideas

6. Compared with cacti, most rain-forest plants
   - ❑ a. have less access to sunlight.
   - ❑ b. have less access to water.
   - ❑ c. require warmer conditions.

7. One can conclude from the article that extreme heat and cold
   - ❑ a. harm all plants.
   - ❑ b. cause most plants to thrive.
   - ❑ c. do not harm well-adapted plants.

8. The article suggests that most plant growth occurs
   - ❑ a. only under extreme conditions.
   - ❑ b. only in temperate and moist regions.
   - ❑ c. when conditions are most favorable.

9. It is likely that deep roots that tapped into underground water supplies would be most useful to plants
   - ❑ a. in the desert.
   - ❑ b. in rain forests.
   - ❑ c. in regions with cold winters.

10. One can infer that a vine with year-round leaves would most likely be found
    - ❑ a. in the Arctic tundra.
    - ❑ b. in cold climates.
    - ❑ c. in the tropical rain forest.

22 B Challenges Facing Coastal Plants

Plants that grow on the Atlantic and Pacific coasts of the United States are well adapted to harsh conditions. They are able to withstand the salt water that soaks into the soil. They also must survive in strong winds and grow in soil that is not very fertile.

Some plants on the coast of New England are able to survive by regulating their salt content. If too much salt gets into a plant, it dries out the plant in a process called dehydration. When the salt content of a seaside plantain gets too high, the salt moves to the leaves and the plant sheds its leaves. Then it grows new leaves. Such fleshy plants as roseroot and goldenrod are able to store fresh water when it rains and later use it to dilute salt water.

Like salt, the wind can cause dehydration in coastal plants. On the Pacific coast, the waxy coating and small size of the leaves of the pickleweed reduce the amount of water lost to the wind. Likewise, the waxy coating of the needles of the Atlantic coast's flagged spruce helps reduce its loss of water through evaporation.

Poor soil is another challenge facing coastal plants. It is difficult for plants to get the nutrients they need in this poor soil. The cobra lily of the Pacific coast, however, obtains needed nutrients from insects that are trapped in a pool of fluid at the base of its leaves.

1. Recognizing Words in Context

Find the word *regulating* in the passage. One definition below is closest to the meaning of that word. One definition has the opposite or nearly opposite meaning. The remaining definition has a completely different meaning. Label the definitions C for *closest,* O for *opposite or nearly opposite,* and D for *different.*

_____ a. growing

_____ b. controlling

_____ c. releasing

2. Distinguishing Fact from Opinion

Two of the statements below present *facts,* which can be proved correct. The other statement is an *opinion,* which expresses someone's thoughts or beliefs. Label the statements F for *fact* and O for *opinion.*

_____ a. Coastal areas present the most difficult growing conditions on Earth.

_____ b. Salt and wind can cause dehydration in plants.

_____ c. Some plants have waxy coatings that protect against water loss from evaporation.

3. Keeping Events in Order

Label the statements below 1, 2, and 3 to show the order in which the events happen.

_____ a. The seaside plantain sheds its leaves.

_____ b. The seaside plantain takes in water that is very salty.

_____ c. Fresh new leaves grow to replace dehydrated ones.

4. Making Correct Inferences

Two of the statements below are correct *inferences,* or reasonable guesses. They are based on information in the passage. The other statement is an incorrect, or faulty, inference. Label the statements C for *correct* inference and F for *faulty* inference.

_____ a. All coastal plants can live for months without fresh water.

_____ b. Coastal plants that have adapted survive in harsh conditions.

_____ c. Plants that grow well in most areas may not grow well in coastal areas.

5. Understanding Main Ideas

One of the statements below expresses the main idea of the passage. One statement is too general, or too broad. The other explains only part of the passage; it is too narrow. Label the statements M for *main idea,* B for *too broad,* and N for *too narrow.*

_____ a. Some plants trap insects to obtain nutrients not found in coastal soil.

_____ b. Coastal plants have adapted to salt water, wind, and poor soil.

_____ c. Some plants have adapted to difficult environments.

Correct Answers, Part A _____

Correct Answers, Part B _____

Total Correct Answers _____

23 A A History of Mountaineering

In mountaineering, a relatively new sport, people climb to the tops of high mountains. Mountaineering probably originated in the Alps, a mountain range in Europe, in the 18th century. Although people have been climbing mountains for thousands of years, in the past they usually did so only if they considered it to be essential to their well being. For example, some ancient peoples climbed to the tops of mountains for religious ceremonies. Others wanted to watch for invading armies. Today, most of the people who make the difficult journey to the top of a high mountain do so just for a feeling of accomplishment.

Mountaineering is a sport of discovery, risk, and competition. To reach the tops of high peaks, climbers must forge paths over steep and often dangerous terrain. They may have to overcome walls of rock and ice, using nothing more than a few tools. Many mountaineers have been killed or seriously injured.

In the early years of the sport, people often were poorly prepared for climbing. Early climbers did not have clothes specially designed for extreme cold, and their only tools were axes for cutting steps into icy terrain. Mountain weather patterns and the effects of high altitudes on the body were not well understood.

Early climbers were intent on learning more about high altitudes. They used thermometers and other devices to learn about mountain weather. In the 19th century, Edward Whymper invented a mountain tent and special climbing tools so that mountaineers might reach even higher peaks. By the late 19th century, mountaineers in the Alps had reached the tops of most of the peaks having heights of 4,000 meters (13,000 feet) or less.

In the 20th century, mountaineers set out to climb the world's highest peaks, some of which rise more than 8,000 meters (26,000 feet). In the early part of the century, climbers used only a few tools and hemp rope. They wore nail-tipped boots for ice climbing and rubber-soled shoes, such as tennis shoes, for rock climbing. By mid-century, lightweight, durable gear—much like the gear used today—had been invented. Climbers began to use oxygen tanks to cope with the thin air at high altitudes. Large expeditions, complete with doctors and fully supplied camps, helped mountaineers reach their goals. By the end of the century, all 14 of the world's 8,000-meter peaks had been climbed. In fact, by 1986 Reinhold Messner had himself climbed all 14 peaks.

Reading Time ______

Recalling Facts

1. The goal of mountaineering is to
   - ❑ a. climb to the tops of high mountains.
   - ❑ b. hike long distances.
   - ❑ c. camp on the sides of mountains for long periods of time.

2. Mountaineering probably originated in the
   - ❑ a. 1700s.
   - ❑ b. 1500s.
   - ❑ c. 1900s.

3. Edward Whymper invented
   - ❑ a. oxygen tanks.
   - ❑ b. a mountain tent.
   - ❑ c. down jackets.

4. One way that mountaineers have tried to deal with the health risks of their sport is by
   - ❑ a. carrying plenty of fresh fruit and vegetables in their packs.
   - ❑ b. going on diets before beginning climbs.
   - ❑ c. taking doctors along on their expeditions.

5. Hemp rope, tools, nail-tipped boots, and tennis shoes were first used by mountaineers in
   - ❑ a. the late 21st century.
   - ❑ b. the early 20th century.
   - ❑ c. ancient times.

Understanding Ideas

6. The article suggests that mountaineers should be
   - ❑ a. willing to buy the most expensive equipment available.
   - ❑ b. in good physical condition and willing to risk death.
   - ❑ c. able to travel to distant parts of the world.

7. From the information in the article, one can infer that mountaineers have the most trouble getting enough oxygen
   - ❑ a. at the highest altitudes.
   - ❑ b. in the Alps.
   - ❑ c. on the coldest mountains.

8. The article suggests that one of the most difficult obstacles that mountaineers encounter is
   - ❑ a. loose soil.
   - ❑ b. hail.
   - ❑ c. ice.

9. Compared with modern mountaineers, early mountaineers
   - ❑ a. reached higher peaks.
   - ❑ b. used clothing and gear that was not very effective.
   - ❑ c. knew more about the mountain weather.

10. One can infer that mountaineering was not popular in ancient times because
    - ❑ a. ancient peoples thought that there were evil spirits on mountaintops.
    - ❑ b. climbing high mountains was dangerous and time consuming.
    - ❑ c. people were waiting for better equipment to be invented.

23 B Learning to Rock Climb

Meera had wanted to go rock climbing with her mother and grandfather for almost a year. But before they acceded to her request, she had had to master the footwork and handholds taught to her on the climbing wall at the local park. Finally, her mother and her grandfather were satisfied. Meera was ready for the real thing.

At the base of a rocky hill in a wilderness area about an hour outside town, Meera put on her rock shoes and waist harness. Grandpa showed Meera how to make a figure-eight knot, and he tied the climbing rope to her harness and to his own. Next, he secured the rope to a nearby anchor. He explained to Meera that she would be the leader, the person climbing the surface, and he would be the belayer, the person in charge of letting out rope as she climbed. Meera's mother would be there to point out holds in the rock if Meera needed help.

As Meera started up the surface, she tried to remember the footwork and handholds she had learned for various rock surfaces. She kept her weight on her feet and used her hands only for stability. Soon, Meera reached a wide ledge and hoisted herself onto it.

"I made it!" Meera shouted to her family below.

Her mother responded, "You've almost made it. Now you have to come down!"

1. Recognizing Words in Context

Find the word *acceded* in the passage. One definition below is closest to the meaning of that word. One definition has the opposite or nearly opposite meaning. The remaining definition has a completely different meaning. Label the definitions C for *closest,* O for *opposite or nearly opposite,* and D for *different.*

______ a. agreed

______ b. refused

______ c. succeeded

2. Distinguishing Fact from Opinion

Two of the statements below present *facts,* which can be proved correct. The other statement is an *opinion,* which expresses someone's thoughts or beliefs. Label the statements F for *fact* and O for *opinion.*

______ a. Rock climbing equipment includes rock shoes, a harness, and rope.

______ b. The belayer is in charge of letting out rope.

______ c. Rock climbing is good for a person's self-esteem.

3. Keeping Events in Order

Label the statements below 1, 2, and 3 to show the order in which the events happen.

______ a. Meera shouts, "I made it!"

______ b. Meera is allowed to go rock climbing with her grandfather and her mother.

______ c. Meera practices climbing on a wall at the park.

4. Making Correct Inferences

Two of the statements below are correct *inferences,* or reasonable guesses. They are based on information in the passage. The other statement is an incorrect, or faulty, inference. Label the statements C for *correct* inference and F for *faulty* inference.

______ a. Rock climbing on a real mountain requires lots of training.

______ b. Most rock climbers eventually suffer injuries.

______ c. Rock climbers should carefully check their equipment before each climb.

5. Understanding Main Ideas

One of the statements below expresses the main idea of the passage. One statement is too general, or too broad. The other explains only part of the passage; it is too narrow. Label the statements M for *main idea,* B for *too broad,* and N for *too narrow.*

______ a. Meera's practice pays off, and she succeeds at her first climb.

______ b. Rock climbing has become a popular form of recreation.

______ c. A figure-eight knot is useful in rock climbing.

Correct Answers, Part A ______

Correct Answers, Part B ______

Total Correct Answers ______

24 A Earth's Rotation

Earth rotates on its axis as it orbits the Sun, completing one full rotation every 24 hours. Earth's axis is an imaginary line that passes through the North Pole and South Pole. As a result of Earth's rotation, regions alternately face the Sun and face away from it, creating a period of daylight and a period of darkness each day. Because different sections of Earth are receiving different amounts of sunlight at any one time, people have divided the world into time zones. When it is daytime on one side of Earth, it is nighttime on the other side of Earth.

The rotation of Earth also creates illusions. People see the Sun in different parts of the sky each day and each night. This view of the heavens gives the impression that the Sun and stars are moving and Earth is not. Actually, the seeming movement of the Sun and stars across the sky is not due to the actual movement of the Sun and stars; it is due almost entirely to the rotation of Earth. Earth's rotation also affects how people perceive the Moon's movements. The Moon appears to move across the sky from east to west like the Sun, but it actually orbits Earth from west to east.

As the Moon orbits Earth, its position in relation to the Sun and Earth causes the moon to appear in different phases. This means that different portions of the Moon are visible on different nights. The light given off by the Moon is reflected light of the Sun. When the Sun is shining directly on the part of the Moon that faces Earth, people see a bright, full moon. When the Sun is shining on the part of the Moon that faces away from Earth, the Moon appears dark and is called a new moon.

When a new moon passes between the Sun and Earth at a certain angle, a solar eclipse occurs. The sunlight shining on the far side of the Moon casts the Moon's shadow on Earth. The Moon blocks the Sun, and the sky grows dark. A lunar eclipse results when Earth is in a particular position directly between the Sun and the Moon. Earth casts its shadow on the Moon, making it appear dark red. Eclipses cannot be seen from regions of Earth's surface that are turned away from the Moon at the time of the eclipse.

Reading Time ______

Recalling Facts

1. Earth completes a full rotation every
   - ❑ a. month.
   - ❑ b. 24 hours.
   - ❑ c. 365 days.

2. The Sun seems to move across the sky because
   - ❑ a. Earth rotates.
   - ❑ b. the Sun orbits Earth.
   - ❑ c. the gravity of Earth pulls on the Sun.

3. The phases of the Moon are caused by the Moon's position in relation to
   - ❑ a. the stars.
   - ❑ b. the ocean.
   - ❑ c. the Sun and Earth.

4. Eclipses result from the position of the
   - ❑ a. Moon in relation to the Sun and Earth.
   - ❑ b. Sun in relation to the stars.
   - ❑ c. Earth in relation to other planets.

5. When the Moon passes between the Sun and Earth at a specific angle, a ______ occurs.
   - ❑ a. full moon
   - ❑ b. lunar eclipse
   - ❑ c. solar eclipse

Understanding Ideas

6. One can conclude from the article that if Earth did not rotate
   - ❑ a. the Moon would not have phases.
   - ❑ b. a solar eclipse would never occur.
   - ❑ c. day and night would not occur in a 24-hour cycle.

7. One can infer that, because the Moon moves through the sky from east to west even though it orbits Earth from west to east,
   - ❑ a. people see a mirror image of the Moon in the sky.
   - ❑ b. Earth rotates much faster than the Moon orbits Earth.
   - ❑ c. the light of the Sun creates an illusion.

8. One can conclude from the article that solar and lunar eclipses
   - ❑ a. both occur when the Moon passes between the Sun and Earth.
   - ❑ b. are visible everywhere.
   - ❑ c. can never occur at the same time.

9. One can infer that a person who sees a half-moon in the sky is seeing
   - ❑ a. a solar eclipse.
   - ❑ b. only half the part of the Moon that the Sun is shining on.
   - ❑ c. a new moon.

10. It is most likely that a solar eclipse would be seen by a person who was
    - ❑ a. jogging in the afternoon.
    - ❑ b. walking in the evening.
    - ❑ c. driving a truck late at night.

24 B Observing the Sun

The Sun is difficult to study because looking directly at it can permanently damage the eyes. As a result, scientists who study the Sun have had to find special ways of observing it. They have developed telescopes and telescope parts that prevent eye damage.

A solar telescope tower at Kitt Peak in Arizona uses mirrors to send an image of the Sun through a 153-meter (500-foot) tube. This allows astronomers to project large, clear images of the Sun. These images can be analyzed in great detail by computerized machines such as spectographs.

Sunspots—dark spots on the Sun's surface—can be viewed by using a standard telescope and a special type of glass screen. The eyepiece of the telescope is removed and replaced with a piece of filtered glass. An image of the Sun with its sunspots appears on the glass piece. A grid inscribed on the glass helps scientists map the sunspots.

The corona, the outermost layer of the Sun's atmosphere, has to be studied in a special way, too. Because the daytime sky is so bright, the corona is not visible under normal conditions. A device called a coronagraph was invented in 1930 to study the corona. It blocks all sunlight except for that which comes from the corona. Today satellite photographs are used to study this and many other aspects of the Sun.

1. Recognizing Words in Context

Find the word *inscribed* in the passage. One definition below is closest to the meaning of that word. One definition has the opposite or nearly opposite meaning. The remaining definition has a completely different meaning. Label the definitions C for *closest,* O for *opposite or nearly opposite,* and D for *different.*

______ a. erased

______ b. melted

______ c. engraved

2. Distinguishing Fact from Opinion

Two of the statements below present *facts,* which can be proved correct. The other statement is an *opinion,* which expresses someone's thoughts or beliefs. Label the statements F for *fact* and O for *opinion.*

______ a. Looking directly at the Sun can damage the eyes.

______ b. Astronomers who study the Sun are braver than other astronomers are.

______ c. Astronomers can use coronagraphs to study the corona of the Sun.

3. Keeping Events in Order

Label the statements below 1, 2, and 3 to show the order in which the events happen.

______ a. The Sun's rays hit the mirrors of the solar telescope.

______ b. Scientists study a large image of the Sun projected by the solar telescope.

______ c. The Sun's rays travel down a long tube on Kitt Peak.

4. Making Correct Inferences

Two of the statements below are correct *inferences,* or reasonable guesses. They are based on information in the passage. The other statement is an incorrect, or faulty, inference. Label the statements C for *correct* inference and F for *faulty* inference.

______ a. Scientists know less about the Sun than they know about other stars.

______ b. Solar telescopes have resulted in the production of much scientific information about the Sun.

______ c. Until the invention of solar telescopes, astronomers spent more time studying the planets than they spent studying the Sun.

5. Understanding Main Ideas

One of the statements below expresses the main idea of the passage. One statement is too general, or too broad. The other explains only part of the passage; it is too narrow. Label the statements M for *main idea,* B for *too broad,* and N for *too narrow.*

______ a. The corona is not visible from Earth under normal conditions.

______ b. With the use of special devices, scientist can study the Sun.

______ c. Scientists use a variety of tools to learn about space.

Correct Answers, Part A ______

Correct Answers, Part B ______

Total Correct Answers ______

25 A Animal Communication

It is a common belief that language is one of the things that makes humans different from animals. Animals have their own complex forms of communication, however. They use scent, body language, and sound to send messages to others of their kind.

Giving off strong-smelling chemicals called pheromones is a powerful way for animals to communicate. They can use the scents of pheromones to attract a mate, signal danger, and recognize locations or family members. Different pheromones have different meanings for a species. Ants use one type of pheromone to make a trail that leads to food and another type to signal an ant's death. Scientists were able to prove how well pheromones work by coating a live ant with the death pheromone. Despite the coated ant's struggles, the other ants carried it out of the nest and discarded it, just as they would a dead ant.

Like ants, bees use pheromone communication to spread messages quickly. In addition to these pheromone messages, bees use a complex pattern of movements, called a dance, to communicate the location of food. When the bee performs this dance for other bees, it vibrates its wings and releases samples of nectar. The others watch the dance and touch the dancing bee to feel its vibrations and taste the nectar. The dance, the vibrations, and the nectar sample relay messages to the bees to direct them to the food source.

Animals as diverse as wolves, cats, and pigeons use other forms of body language. The wag of a wolf's tail signals a greeting; the arched back and erect tail of a cat signal its threat to attack. In contrast, some birds, such as peacocks and pigeons, use body language to attract a mate. A peacock spreads its tail into a wide fan, and a male pigeon puffs the feathers on its chest to catch the attention of females.

Animals also communicate by using sounds. The sounds of a particular animal may vary by region. Some animals use sounds that humans can hear, whereas bats and other animals use sounds that humans cannot hear. Male humpback whales communicate with patterns of clicks, creaks, and groans that scientists call songs. Some of the sounds are louder than a jet airliner. Scientists think the songs may involve claims to territory in breeding areas, but there is much about these and other animal sounds that is yet to be understood.

Reading Time ______

Recalling Facts

1. One of the ways in which many animals communicate is with
   - ❑ a. speech.
   - ❑ b. scent.
   - ❑ c. sign language.
2. A pheromone is a type of
   - ❑ a. bee.
   - ❑ b. chemical.
   - ❑ c. high-pitched sound.
3. To direct other bees to a food source, a bee
   - ❑ a. brings a group of bees from its hive to the site.
   - ❑ b. uses buzzing sounds to tell the location.
   - ❑ c. performs a dance.
4. When an ant dies underground, other ants
   - ❑ a. eat it.
   - ❑ b. carry it out of the nest.
   - ❑ c. use it as fertilizer.
5. An animal that communicates with clicks and groans is
   - ❑ a. a humpbacked whale.
   - ❑ b. a bat.
   - ❑ c. an elephant.

Understanding Ideas

6. The article suggests that, as a result of increased knowledge of animal communication,
   - ❑ a. humans can communicate with almost any animal.
   - ❑ b. animals are not attacking humans as often as in the past.
   - ❑ c. scientists have gained knowledge about animal behavior.
7. If a mammal wanted to help its mate find a certain location in the future, it would most likely use
   - ❑ a. scent.
   - ❑ b. body language.
   - ❑ c. sound.
8. The article suggests that whales have a highly developed form of communication because
   - ❑ a. they can make loud sounds.
   - ❑ b. fish do not understand their communication system.
   - ❑ c. their sounds are arranged in patterns.
9. One can infer that bees communicate with complicated dances because they
   - ❑ a. are more intelligent than other insects.
   - ❑ b. must give directions to locations that may be far away.
   - ❑ c. they lack pheromones.
10. The form of communication most likely to be understood by different types of creatures is
    - ❑ a. sound.
    - ❑ b. body language.
    - ❑ c. chemical messages.

25 B

Can Animals Communicate with People?

In the late 1940s, two scientists began a project to teach a chimpanzee named Viki to speak. Viki learned to say just four words, and the study failed. But a crucial lesson in human-animal communication was learned. Instead of expecting animals to communicate in the same way that humans do, scientists learned to take into account the inborn skills of animals. Because of the structure of their vocal tracts, chimps are not able to make many common human sounds.

In the 1960s, scientists began to teach some chimps and gorillas American Sign Language, or ASL, to communicate through signs. A chimp named Washoe and a gorilla named Koko were able to learn hundreds of signs taught by the humans who raised them.

Some experts question the usefulness of these projects. They believe that the animals are not learning language but instead are learning to imitate their owners. Washoe, however, has shown some sophisticated communication strategies. Upon seeing a swan for the first time, Washoe used the signs for *water* and *bird* to describe it. When Koko was tested by a stranger and asked to make the signs for each of a series of objects, she was right 60 percent of the time. This rate of success was much higher than the one resulting from random guessing. Incidents like these seem to suggest that primates and other intelligent animals have some ability for language.

1. Recognizing Words in Context

Find the word *sophisticated* in the passage. One definition below is closest to the meaning of that word. One definition has the opposite or nearly opposite meaning. The remaining definition has a completely different meaning. Label the definitions C for *closest,* O for *opposite or nearly opposite,* and D for *different.*

______ a. developed

______ b. incorrect

______ c. crude

2. Distinguishing Fact from Opinion

Two of the statements below present *facts,* which can be proved correct. The other statement is an *opinion,* which expresses someone's thoughts or beliefs. Label the statements F for *fact* and O for *opinion.*

______ a. Washoe and Koko have learned hundreds of signs.

______ b. Chimps cannot make many common human sounds.

______ c. Animals are smarter than people think.

3. **Keeping Events in Order**
Label the statements below 1, 2, and 3 to show the order in which the events happened.

_____ a. Scientists found that chimps cannot copy much human speech.

_____ b. Scientists started teaching a chimp sign language.

_____ c. A chimp named Viki learned to say only four words.

4. **Making Correct Inferences**
Two of the statements below are correct *inferences,* or reasonable guesses. They are based on information in the passage. The other statement is an incorrect, or faulty, inference. Label the statements C for *correct* inference and F for *faulty* inference.

_____ a. In spite of some experts' doubts, animals appear to be capable of some aspects of language.

_____ b. All languages require that words be placed in an exact order.

_____ c. At one time, people thought animals could be taught to speak as humans speak.

5. **Understanding Main Ideas**
One of the statements below expresses the main idea of the passage. One statement is too general, or too broad. The other explains only part of the passage; it is too narrow. Label the statements M for *main idea,* B for *too broad,* and N for *too narrow.*

_____ a. Chimpanzees cannot make many common human sounds.

_____ b. Humans have been able to teach animals some complex skills.

_____ c. Some animals have shown that they have some ability to communicate with signs.

Correct Answers, Part A _____

Correct Answers, Part B _____

Total Correct Answers _____

Answer Key

Reading Rate Graph

Comprehension Score Graph

Comprehension Skills Profile Graph

ANSWER KEY

1A	1. b	2. a	3. c	4. a	5. c	6. b	7. a	8. b	9. c	10. c
1B	1. O, C, D		2. F, O, F		3. 2, 3, 1		4. C, F, C		5. M, B, N	
2A	1. a	2. b	3. c	4. b	5. c	6. b	7. a	8. a	9. b	10. a
2B	1. D, C, O		2. F, F, O		3. S, A, S		4. F, C, C		5. N, B, M	
3A	1. c	2. a	3. b	4. a	5. c	6. c	7. c	8. a	9. c	10. a
3B	1. O, D, C		2. O, F, F		3. 2, 3, 1		4. C, F, C		5. N, B, M	
4A	1. b	2. a	3. c	4. c	5. a	6. b	7. a	8. b	9. c	10. c
4B	1. C, D, O		2. F, F, O		3. 1, 3, 2		4. C, C, F		5. M, N, B	
5A	1. c	2. a	3. b	4. a	5. a	6. c	7. b	8. c	9. a	10. c
5B	1. C, O, D		2. F, F, O		3. S, B, S		4. F, C, C		5. N, M, B	
6A	1. a	2. c	3. a	4. b	5. c	6. b	7. a	8. c	9. c	10. a
6B	1. D, O, C		2. O, F, F		3. 2, 1, 3		4. C, C, F		5. N, M, B	
7A	1. b	2. b	3. a	4. c	5. c	6. a	7. b	8. b	9. b	10. c
7B	1. O, D, C		2. O, F, F		3. 2, 1, 3		4. C, F, C		5. B, N, M	
8A	1. c	2. a	3. b	4. b	5. c	6. a	7. c	8. a	9. c	10. b
8B	1. D, O, C		2. F, O, F		3. S, B, S		4. C, F, C		5. M, N, B	
9A	1. b	2. a	3. b	4. c	5. a	6. a	7. c	8. c	9. c	10. b
9B	1. O, C, D		2. F, O, F		3. 2, 1, 3		4. F, C, C		5. N, M, B	
10A	1. a	2. b	3. a	4. c	5. a	6. c	7. c	8. b	9. b	10. a
10B	1. D, O, C		2. O, F, F		3. 2, 1, 3		4. F, C, C		5. B, N, M	
11A	1. c	2. a	3. c	4. a	5. a	6. c	7. b	8. a	9. a	10. c
11B	1. O, C, D		2. F, F, O		3. 3, 2, 1		4. F, C, C		5. B, M, N	
12A	1. c	2. c	3. b	4. a	5. b	6. c	7. a	8. c	9. a	10. c
12B	1. C, D, O		2. F, O, F		3. 3, 1, 2		4. F, C, C		5. N, M, B	
13A	1. a	2. a	3. c	4. b	5. b	6. c	7. a	8. c	9. a	10. b
13B	1. D, O, C		2. F, F, O		3. 3, 2, 1		4. C, F, C		5. B, N, M	

14A	1. b	2. a	3. c	4. b	5. a	6. b	7. b	8. a	9. c	10. b
14B	1. C, D, O		2. F, F, O		3. 2, 1, 3		4. C, C, F		5. N, M, B	
15A	1. c	2. a	3. a	4. b	5. b	6. a	7. c	8. b	9. a	10. b
15B	1. O, C, D		2. O, F, F		3. 1, 3, 2		4. C, C, F		5. M, N, B	
16A	1. b	2. a	3. a	4. c	5. b	6. b	7. a	8. c	9. b	10. a
16B	1. D, O, C		2. F, O, F		3. S, S, A		4. F, C, C		5. B, N, M	
17A	1. c	2. c	3. b	4. a	5. b	6. c	7. a	8. b	9. b	10. a
17B	1. D, C, O		2. O, F, F		3. 2, 3, 1		4. C, C, F		5. M, B, N	
18A	1. b	2. c	3. a	4. c	5. a	6. a	7. b	8. b	9. a	10. a
18B	1. C, O, D		2. F, O, F		3. S, S, B		4. C, C, F		5. M, N, B	
19A	1. b	2. a	3. b	4. c	5. a	6. b	7. b	8. c	9. a	10. b
19B	1. D, C, O		2. F, F, O		3. 3, 1, 2		4. F, C, C		5. B, N, M	
20A	1. a	2. a	3. b	4. c	5. b	6. a	7. b	8. c	9. a	10. b
20B	1. O, C, D		2. F, O, F		3. 1, 3, 2		4. C, C, F		5. M, N, B	
21A	1. c	2. a	3. b	4. a	5. b	6. b	7. a	8. b	9. a	10. b
21B	1. O, C, D		2. F, F, O		3. 2, 3, 1		4. C, F, C		5. B, N, M	
22A	1. b	2. a	3. c	4. a	5. c	6. a	7. c	8. c	9. a	10. c
22B	1. D, C, O		2. O, F, F		3. 2, 1, 3		4. F, C, C		5. N, M, B	
23A	1. a	2. a	3. b	4. c	5. b	6. b	7. a	8. c	9. b	10. b
23B	1. C, O, D		2. F, F, O		3. 3, 2, 1		4. C, F, C		5. M, B, N	
24A	1. b	2. a	3. c	4. a	5. c	6. c	7. b	8. c	9. b	10. a
24B	1. O, D, C		2. F, O, F		3. 1, 3, 2		4. F, C, C		5. N, M, B	
25A	1. b	2. b	3. c	4. b	5. a	6. c	7. a	8. c	9. b	10. b
25B	1. C, D, O		2. F, F, O		3. 3, 1, 2		4. C, F, C		5. N, B, M	

Reading Rate

Put an X on the line above each lesson number to show your reading time and words-per-minute rate for that lesson.

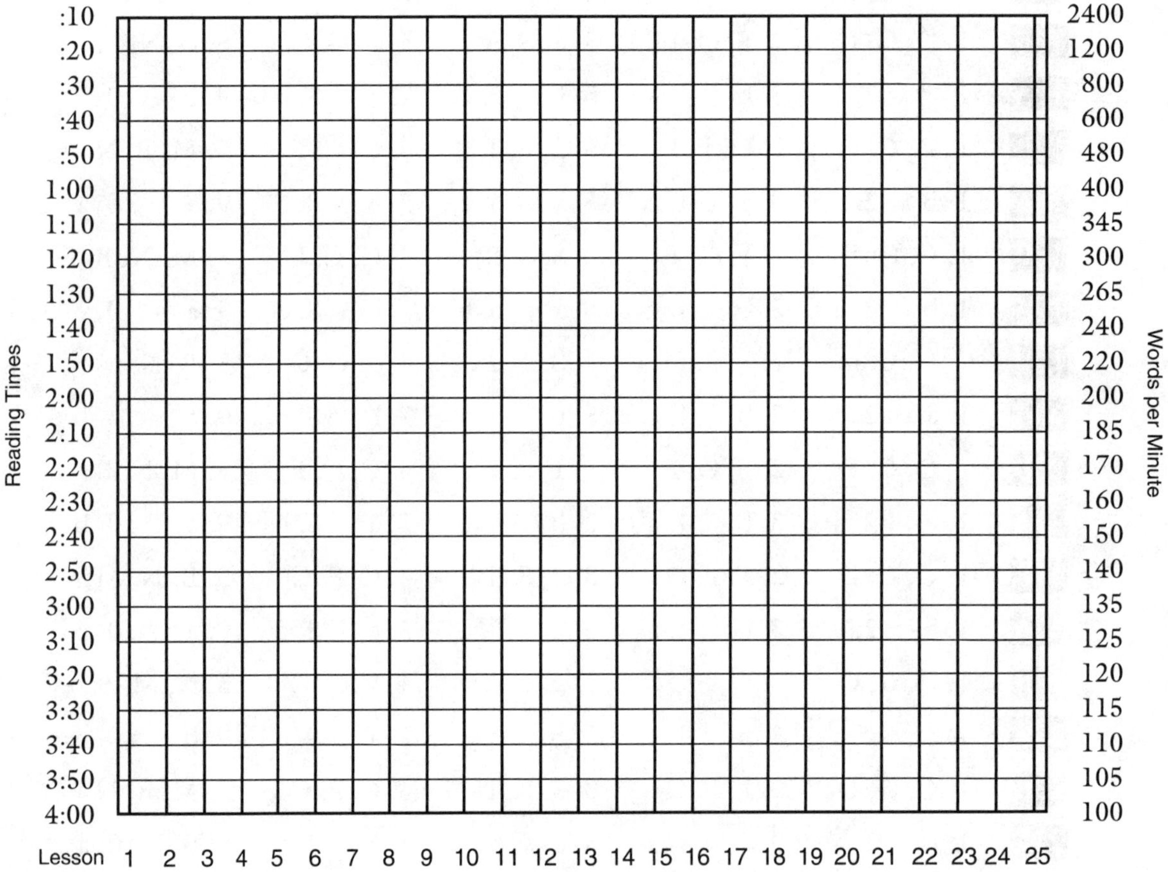

Comprehension Score

Put an X on the line above each lesson number to indicate your total correct answers and comprehension score for that lesson.

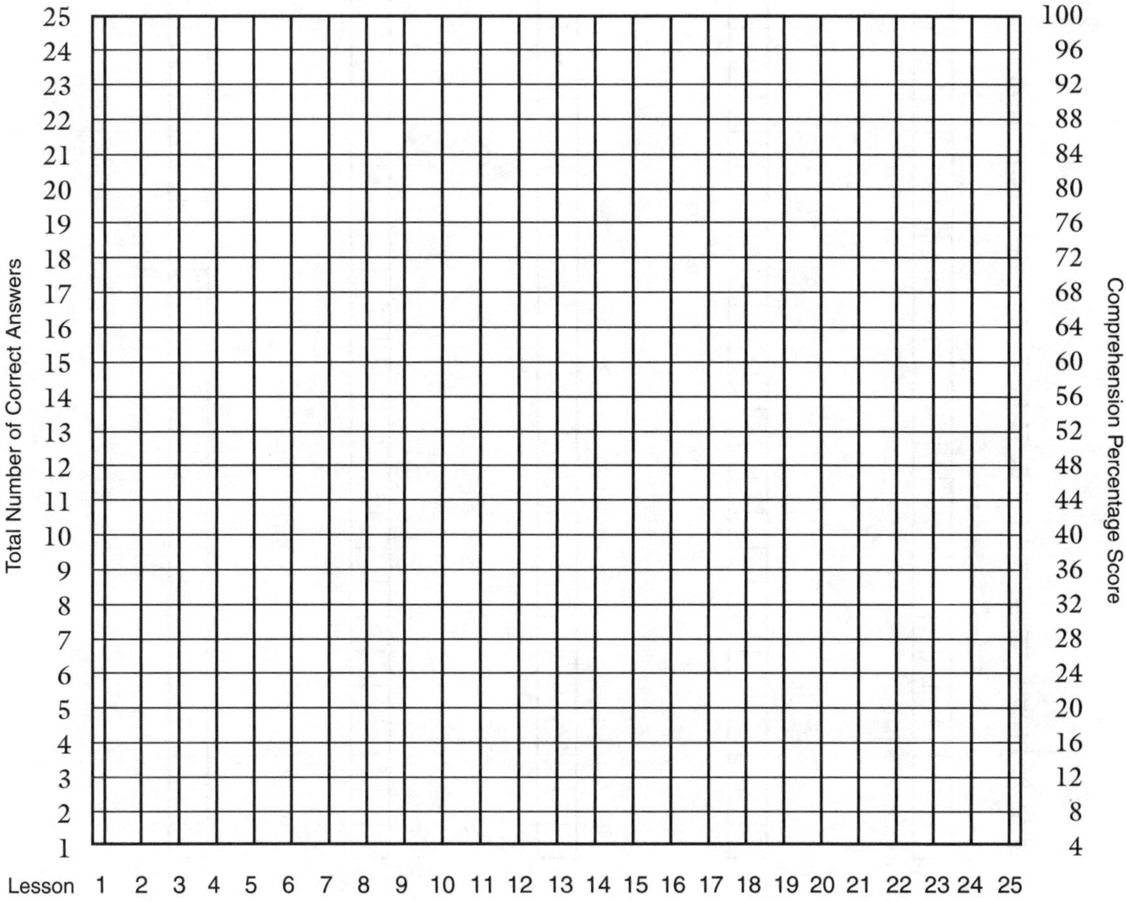

Comprehension Skills Profile

Put an X in the box above each question type to indicate an incorrect reponse to any part of that question.

	Recognizing Words in Context	Distinguishing Fact from Opinion	Keeping Events in Order	Making Correct Inferences	Understanding Main Ideas
Lesson 1					
2					
3					
4					
5					
6					
7					
8					
9					
10					
11					
12					
13					
14					
15					
16					
17					
18					
19					
20					
21					
22					
23					
24					
25					